PORTRAITS IN
COURAGE

Resources by Dave Dravecky

Comeback (with Tim Stafford)
When You Can't Come Back (with Ken Gire)
The Worth of a Man (with C. W. Neal)
The Worth of a Man audio

Resources by Jan Dravecky

A Joy I'd Never Known (with Connie Neal)
A Joy I'd Never Known audio

Resources by Dave and Jan Dravecky

Do Not Lose Heart (with Steve Halliday)
Glimpses of Heaven (with Amanda Sorenson)
Portraits in Courage (with Steve Halliday)
Stand by Me (with Amanda Sorenson)

Extraordinary Lessons *from* Everyday Heroes

PORTRAITS IN
COURAGE

DAVE & JAN
DRAVECKY

with STEVE HALLIDAY

ZondervanPublishingHouse
Grand Rapids, Michigan

A Division of HarperCollinsPublishers

Portraits in Courage
Copyright © 1998 by David and Janice Dravecky

Requests for information should be addressed to:

 ZondervanPublishingHouse
Grand Rapids, Michigan 49530

Library of Congress Cataloging-in-Publication Data

Dravecky, Dave.
    Portraits in courage : extraordinary lessons from everyday heroes / Dave
and Jan Dravecky with Steve Halliday.
       p.   cm.
    ISBN 0-310-21664-8 (pbk. : alk. paper)
    1. Courage—Religious aspects—Christianity.   2. Cancer—Patients—
Religious live 3. Christian biography. I. Dravecky, Jan. II. Halliday,
Steve, 1957-   . III. Title.
BV4647.C75D73 1998
248.8'6'0922—dc21   98-24703
   [B]   CIP

All Scripture quotations, unless otherwise indicated, are taken from the *Holy Bible:
New International Version*®. NIV®. Copyright © 1973, 1978, 1984 by International
Bible Society. Used by permission of Zondervan Publishing House. All rights
reserved.

Published in association with the literary agency of Alive Communications, Inc.,
1465 Kelly Johnson Blvd., Suite 320, Colorado Springs, CO 80920.

Interior design by Sherri Hoffman

Printed in the United States of America

---

98 99 00 01 02 03 04 /❖ DC/ 10 9 8 7 6 5 4 3 2 1

CONTENTS

PART THREE: THE STRENGTH TO DIE

INTRODUCTION:
Everyday People, Extraordinary Courage

For good reason the 1939 film classic *The Wizard of Oz* has enchanted and dazzled generations of movie fans the world over. It brought to Technicolor life the lovable characters first created at the turn of the century by children's author L. Frank Baum. Who can forget Dorothy and her little dog Toto, or the Tin Man, or the Scarecrow, or the Wicked Witch of the West?

For my money, however, the most memorable character of all will always remain the Cowardly Lion—a fumbling, frightened feline in need of a healthy dose of courage.

One scene from the movie especially stands out in my memory. Right before Dorothy and her ragtag collection of misfits are scheduled to appear before the great and dreadful Oz—the supposedly all-powerful wizard and ruler of this magic land—the Lion holds court and declares what he hopes to receive from the great man:

> Friends: Your Majesty, if you were king, you wouldn't be afraid of anything?
> Lion: Not nobody! Not no how!
> Friends: Not even a rhinoceros?
> Lion: Imposserous!
> Friends: How about a hippopotamus?
> Lion: Why, I'd thrash him from top to bottomus!
> Friends: Supposin' you met an elephant?
> Lion: I'd wrap him up in cellophant!
> Friends: What if it were a brontosaurus?
> Lion: I'd show *him* who was King of the Forest!
> Friends: How?

> Lion: How? Courage! What makes a king out of a slave?
> Courage. What makes a flag on the mast to wave?
> Courage. What makes the elephant charge his tusk,
> in the misty mist or the dusky dusk? What makes
> the muskrat guard his musk? Courage. What makes
> the Sphinx the Seventh wonder? Courage. What
> makes the dawn come up like thunder? Courage.
> What makes the Hottentots so hot? What puts the
> ape in apricot? What do they got that I ain't got?
>
> Friends: Courage.
>
> Lion: You can say that again. *Huh???*

That scene never fails to bring a smile to my face—but the truth is, the Cowardly Lion isn't the only one in need of a good shot of courage. Life has a way of making cowards of us all. Who among us doesn't need a new infusion of courage every now and then?

Such a conviction apparently gripped the mind of the young John F. Kennedy when in the mid-1950s he spent six months strapped to a board at his father's house in Palm Beach, Florida, after undergoing serious back surgery. Kennedy used his recuperation time to write the stories of eight American political leaders who, for conscience' sake, had defied popular opinion. His efforts resulted in the book *Profiles In Courage*, which won the Pulitzer Prize in 1957.

Courage. We all want it. We all need it. But when life grows difficult, why does it seem so hard to find? How can we gain the courage we need at the very times it seems most elusive?

I think Kennedy had the right idea—you tell the inspiring stories of courageous men and women who already walked this path. You describe what they were up against: the stormy oceans they had to sail, the craggy mountains they had to climb, the dark valleys they had to cross . . . and you show by their example how we can do the same.

Kennedy profiled eight political heroes, but courage is not confined to the political arena. Stories of incredible courage come from all walks of life and extend into every nook and cranny of human existence. And I believe courage grows best in the soil of our own hearts when we hear about ordinary men and women who display extraordinary courage, even in the howling wilderness of staggering personal pain.

Hence this book. I want to recount the stories of everyday people caught in trials who somehow found the strength to live courageously. I want to bring comfort to those who are suffering now by showing them they are not alone on this painful path. Others before them also walked this fiery road, yet they struck out on their fearsome journey with courage and faith. You can do the same.

While a majority of these stories concern people battling cancer, this book is not about cancer. You or someone you love may not be fighting cancer, but the lessons and experiences of the brave people chronicled in this book can nevertheless be a tremendous encouragement to you. Suffering transcends any particular disease and affects every aspect of life. The lessons we learn from those who are suffering—whatever kind of suffering that may be—can strengthen and encourage us, regardless of our own experiences.

(Our purpose at the Outreach of Hope is to come alongside men and women, boys and girls, who are struggling with cancer or amputation; and since most of the stories in this book come out of our ministry, they reflect the struggles of the people we serve.)

The people you are about to meet in the following pages all have one thing in common: they faced (or are facing) the excruciating adversities of life with undaunted courage. As you read their stories, imagine that you are walking down the hallways of Dave Dravecky's personal "Hall of Faith." On the walls hang many inspiring portraits of ordinary men and women who gained their honored place in the hall by the way in which they responded to the worst hardships life could throw at them.

My hall has three wings, first suggested to me by German theologian Jurgen Moltmann. He once told a group of deaconesses caring for disabled people that "health is not a condition of my body; it is the power of my soul to cope with the varying condition of my body." True health, he said, "is the *strength to live*, the *strength to suffer* and the *strength to die*" (italics mine).

The wing in my hall labeled "The Strength to Live" features the portraits of ten men and women who choose to live life to the full, despite their enormous challenges and deep pain. They refuse to give up on living. Instead, they look within and to God for the strength to keep going.

After leaving this first wing you'll enter another, this one called "The Strength to Suffer." There you will gaze upon the striking portraits of ten extraordinary people whose suffering is so great they cannot carry on life "as normal"—but neither do they live as though the grave already had swallowed them whole. They teach us not only how to suffer with courage and grace, but also enable us to peek beneath the thick veil of scorching pain to reveal wonders not visible to eyes never awash in tears.

I have no doubt you'll know when you have entered the third and final wing of my hall; its light is noticeably subdued. The chiseled words, "The Strength to Die," stand guard over the ten portraits enshrined here—but this is not a somber place! Death may be the final enemy, but it is *not* the final victor. And the portraits hanging in this wing demonstrate that truth with passion and even joy.

I suggest you stroll through these halls slowly, taking in and pondering each portrait thoughtfully. Perhaps it would be best to read one story a day rather than trying to digest whole sections at a time.

As you prepare to walk through this very personal Hall of Faith, remember that the men and women honored here—their faces creased with deep pain, yet their spirits uncrushed by the worst life has to offer—are, like most of us, *ordinary*. They're not heads of state. They're not Nobel laureates. They're not war heroes or media superstars or billionaire entrepreneurs. They're ordinary men and women who have found the extraordinary courage to live out their days as a blessing to others and a tribute to their God. I know most of these people personally; their paths crossed mine somewhere along the way and I have been amazingly blessed from the encounter.

And I think you will be, too.

Dave Dravecky
Colorado Springs, Colorado

PART ONE

THE STRENGTH TO LIVE

1

WITH OR WITHOUT

Some people really know how to live—even when others think they shouldn't. Shouldn't live, that is. Judy Squier has faced that kind of hostility head-on and has overcome it remarkably. She does so by focusing not on what she can't do, but on what she can.

"With the red light flashing in my rear view mirror," Judy Squier says with a twinkle in her eye, "it was obvious—the ticket had my name on it. I pulled off the road, opened my window and strained to hear the officer's words over the loud beats of my heart.

"'You ran the stop sign,' he said, peering down at me. 'May I see your driver's license?'

"Instantly I pictured my forgotten purse, lying forlornly on the couch at home. I winced as I answered, 'Can I go get my wallet real fast? I live two minutes from here.'

"Without any change of expression the officer flipped open his icy silver clipboard and demanded, 'Your name?'

"'Judith Ann Squier,' I meekly replied.

"'Your address?'

"'4113 Alpine Road.'

"'Your weight?'

"This one I couldn't resist. Sitting tall but feeling short, I asked, 'With or without my legs?'"

It's a question Judy has been asking since she was ten years old, after doctors at Shriner's Hospital in Chicago amputated her congenitally deformed feet and fit her with twin prostheses.

Judy was born March 4, 1945—a very bad day in the eyes of the obstetrician who brought her into the world. "Your daughter is going to live,

15

I am sorry to say," he announced to Judy's startled parents. Yet despite the man's wretched outlook, God had his hand on Judy's life from the very beginning. Even her name means "Praise," a fact her mother did not know when she chose the name.

"What a comfort to know God's foot was in the door, particularly since I was born with no lower limbs and a deformed hand," Judy says today. That's one reason why Psalm 139:15,16 is especially precious to her. "You were there while I was being formed in utter seclusion," writes the psalmist. "You saw me before I was born and scheduled each day of my life" (LIVING BIBLE).

Judy will always be grateful to her older sister, Tina, whom she describes as "an eternal helper and friend." Tina included her legless sister in all kinds of activities—tree climbing, plunging off high dives, riding bikes. Not that Judy was without means of locomotion! She walked on metal stilts until she was ten, when she received her first set of artificial limbs. "Long legs, bending knees, full size feet, I loved every inch of them," she says. "No matter that they were hollow, hewn willow wood, not skin and bones."

Once the new prostheses were hers, she immediately bolted for the shoe store, returning home with ten pairs of shoes. Soon afterwards a red Schwinn bike with her name on it sat ready to propel her into new adventures. Judy was determined to live as expansively as possible, yet she never could forget her handicap. Her first speech, prepared and given at age thirteen, was titled, "Learning to Walk on Artificial Limbs."

"I joined the legs crowd," Judy says, "but I quickly discovered I couldn't keep up with them. Walking was work. I couldn't run, skip, jump rope, jitterbug, water-ski or climb or descend stairs with ease or speed like my sister. So my love affair with my prostheses waned."

Her father, on the other hand, made it his practice every day before sunrise to make sure his daughter was fully dressed—and that included prostheses. On the night she was to be confirmed at church, Judy dressed, leaving her artificial limbs leaning against the wall, and then started to crawl down the stairs on her stumps. "You will not go to your confirmation tonight without your legs!" bellowed her dad. She pouted but obeyed, slinking back upstairs to her room to put on her wooden legs. The family arrived too late for the program—but not too late for Judy to *walk* down the aisle to be confirmed! "I walked steadily forward on my earthly father's determination," she confesses.

By age fifteen Judy's own determination kicked in. She became a junior counselor at a camp for the physically disabled, caring for cerebral palsied children in wheelchairs. In high school Judy remembers being invited to a military ball, where she felt like Cinderella in her lovely pink gown. "But I wasn't afraid I'd lose a slipper," she admits. "I was afraid I'd lose a leg!"

Experiences like the one at the ball awakened in Judy some deep desires she never expected to be fulfilled.

"I still remember looking out the window of my dad's car on a cold, wintry night, and dreaming an impossible dream," she says. "My heart whispered, 'Star light, star bright, first star I've seen tonight—I wish I may, I wish I might have the wish I wish tonight. I wish for a husband . . . somehow, someday.'"

Judy had no way of knowing it, but within 100 miles of that lonely country road where she mouthed her silent wish lived a boy named David Squier who in a few years would grow up to become the man of her dreams. Judy likes to say that she received her MA degree in Speech Pathology the same month she received her Mrs. degree. On her wedding day she moved to California to begin her new life as Mrs. David Squier and to start her career as a speech pathologist. Judy's impossible dream had become reality.

It never was her dream, however, to become a mother. Judy was fearful that any children of hers would share her disabilities and therefore put the thought out of her mind. Judy remembers saying hundreds of times, "There are two things in life I never want to do: Have a root canal or have a baby." But ten years after her marriage she discovered the second of those desires was about to be trampled forever. "OK, doctor," she said when she heard the news, "I'm pregnant. What I wonder is: do I deliver a baby with my legs on or off?" Two weeks before the due date she found the answer to her question. Labor came so quickly that firemen had to be called to retrieve her, and the Squiers' first daughter, Emily, was born six minutes after Judy arrived at Stanford Emergency. And her artificial legs stayed home by the nightstand.

Two more daughters, Elizabeth and Naphtalie Joy, joined the family within five years. Through trial and error Judy quickly learned how to go about baby-caring tasks. For nursing, diaper changing, and bathing, Judy set up both high and low stations so she could be with or without legs. Yet inevitably there were mishaps.

"One of my earliest memories was walking out of the library and watching my mother fall to the ground," Emily reported. "Her artificial limb broke in half. I was too young to help, so I just stood there and screamed. Finally a stranger lifted Mom into our minivan. We headed off to the leg man, who glued Mom's leg back together."

Throughout her childhood, Emily served as the helper Judy needed. At four, Emily learned to help carry her baby sister. As she grew older Emily learned to load her mother's heavy wheelchair into the van and to bounce the wheelchair down stairs and push it up steep hills. "I have learned how much joy one can have in every good and bad situation in life, because joy is overflowing from my mom," Emily declared. "I have learned how God can show his power in our weakness if we allow him, because I have seen God's power work in my mom's weakness."

In the summer of 1997, Emily visited Guatemala to work with severely disabled/neglected kids living in the city of Antigua. One day she fed a helpless boy confined to a crib; his immobile legs hung limp as he sat and stared off into space. When Emily returned home and told her mother the story, Judy replied, "I was that little child. You were feeding me." Judy then recounted her earliest childhood memory—feelings of intense loneliness as she lay in a crib at Shriner's Hospital. "Mom may not have legs to run around and jump up and down, but God gave her strong spiritual limbs and a heart of gold," Emily says. "God is the one who has changed her lonely life to what it is now."

Through her growing daughters, Judy managed to vicariously enjoy running, skipping, jumping rope, water skiing, and doing backflips and front walkovers. Today Emily is a cross country runner, while Betsy and Naphtalie are gymnasts. A good friend has watched all this happen and one day told Judy, "What a good God we have, Judy. You were born with no legs and now you have six good ones."

Of course, that's the upside of this story. The downside also exists.

"Let's face it," Judy says, "I've seen life from down under. Amid all my blessings, I could instantly name three major entries on my List of Low Points: Finding out I was different; Facing daily those things I can't do; Having to wait and/or rely on others to do for me what my mind has already done but my body can't. Seven days a week I wrestle an opponent who snarls, 'You're a loser!' I see myself the little crippled girl, the handicapped Pied Piper with an entourage of neighborhood kids staring and mimicking my penguin-like gait through the aisles of our corner grocery store. I see myself a teenager sitting legless on my sister's bed, watching her ready herself for the Friday night sock hop. And I see a tired mom needing encouragement one Sunday when an acquaintance asked, 'How's it going, Judy?' Discouraged, I dumped my whole week of frustrations and talked of trying to mother three children under five years of age while clumping along on two artificial limbs instead of healthy, strong legs—and heard the heartless retort, 'You're not a special case. Mothering is impossible PERIOD.'"

Judy would never have chosen a life without legs, but she believes her disability has enriched her life in ways she might never have experienced otherwise. The day that church acquaintance gave her such an insensitive reply, for example, she saw three things happen. First, her self pity was dealt a death blow. Second, she recognized how far short all humans fall in fulfilling life's duties. And third, she heard a still, small voice lovingly whisper to her, "Whatever you lack, I am." "Being born without legs has brought me to my knees," she says.

In November 1991 Judy was honored in Washington, D.C., as one of three handicapped Americans whose lives demonstrate family strength. To commemorate the honor she received a fifteen pound bronze statue depicting a strong eagle in flight, bringing food to its nest of eaglets. She keeps the statue at home, right next to the orthopedic baby shoe—scratched and worn with rivets that once connected it to her metal stilts—that her parents had bronzed. She's not sure which "statue" means the most.

And what is the secret of Judy's remarkable ability, not only to cope, but to thrive? She traces that secret to August 14, 1965, the day she accepted Christ into her heart. "For years I looked forward to receiving 'real legs' in heaven one day," she said. "I thought how grand it would be to climb a mountain, to feel sand between my toes, to do a cartwheel. But after fifty years, most of those having walked with the Lord, my focus has changed. My heart longs to see his face. And I will count it a supreme privilege to spend eternity sitting at his feet."

2

TURNING SETBACKS
INTO COMEBACKS

You don't have to be a professional athlete to turn a setback into a comeback. That, at least, has been the life message of Ron Gustafson ever since he lost his right arm and shoulder in a farm accident on September, 1975, as a nine-year-old fourth grader from Lyons, Nebraska. Ron was helping his dad with farm chores when the tractor's rear axle broke and fell on him, cutting off his right arm and shoulder. The mishap also severely damaged his right leg; for several years doctors weren't sure they could save it, and by Ron's sophomore year in high school the leg already had undergone fourteen corrective operations.

Despite his obvious handicaps, Ron never thought for a moment about giving up. He always drove himself to become the best he could be. Let me take you back through time to see what newspaper reporters and columnists had to say about this amazing kid as he pursued his "impossible" athletic dreams.

October 23, 1975[1]

Ronny Gustafson returned home Saturday after spending nearly six weeks in the hospital at Fremont following a tractor accident near his parent's farm.

Ronny has a golf cart to help him get around outside.

Sunday afternoon Ronny was the center of attention at the Port of the Grounded Grouse (the Lyons airport) as he was driving up and down the runway in his cart. A large crowd gathered at the airport to welcome Ronny home and to tell him how proud everyone is of his attitude and the way he has battled back after the accident.

Monday evening Ronny got to go to the Lyons JV and freshman football game. He sat on a mattress in the back of a station wagon and watched the games.

Ronny has been keeping active since his return home. Tuesday he wanted to try his hand at shooting a few baskets. So his dad, Don, fixed a protective device around Ronny's leg so the basketball wouldn't hit the leg, and Ronny shot baskets while sitting in his cart. His mother, Joyce, reported that Ronny made one basket during his work-out. . . .

Ronny remains in good spirits, despite the ordeal he has been through these past six weeks. During the six week hospital stay, Ronny had surgery nine times.

October 23, 1975[2]

This week's column is dedicated to Ronny Gustafson. If there was ever a more courageous and inspirational young man, we would certainly like to meet him. . . . Even in the ambulance on the way to the hospital he talked about how he would still be able to participate in sports, which is such a big part of his young life. And he has not changed that goal one little bit. And do you know he has made believers out of everyone? We really believe that someday Ronny will again be active in school sports just like his classmates. . . .

August 9, 1977[3]

Pee wee no-hitters are a dime a dozen . . . fifteen cents at the most. Nothing unusual about a no-hitter in pee wees. Certainly nothing worth mentioning in a column, right?

Well, that's where you're wrong.

A young Lyons athlete, Ronny Gustafson, deserves special citation here. Gustafson pitched two no-hitters this season . . . two solid gold no-hitters.

What makes his feat so noteworthy is that he has only one arm, the left. And until losing his right arm in a terrible farm accident Sept. 2, 1975, he was a right-hander.

"Ronny Gustafson has more courage than anybody I've ever known, and that includes adults. He's absolutely one of a kind. He's remarkable. He's . . . well, golly, there just are not words to describe the kind of kid he is," said Jerry Mathers of Lyons, Ronny's fourth-grade teacher and one who has taken special interest in and spent time with the youngest son of the Don Gustafsons of rural Lyons. . . . "He was, without the slightest doubt, the greatest young right-handed thrower I've ever seen," Mathers said. . . .

In order to fully understand the depth of young Mr. Gustafson's 360-degree turn, you have to appreciate his incredible ability as a right-handed pee wee. He was a phenom. "Ever since he was seven he played with the eleven-to-twelve age group in Lyons because he was too big, too good and threw too fast for his own age group," brother Rick said. . . . [But then] the phenom was suddenly without his strong, talented right arm . . . and almost without his right leg. "He never once moped about it or felt sorry for himself. He went right to work on making the most of the one arm and the one good leg he had left. On his very first day home from the hospital he was tying his shoelaces all by himself left-handed. And after he got his shoelaces on he went out and shot baskets," Rick Gustafson said.

The idea of switching positions after he lost his right arm never entered his mind.

"That's all he ever wanted to be, and the accident didn't change his mind. My brothers and dad and I set up a mattress, some posts, a plate, pitching rubber and a bucket of balls, and he went right to work. He was determined to be as good left-handed as he ever was right-handed. It was a sight to behold . . . his perseverance, determination, guts, desire. We just loved him for it," said the oldest Gustafson brother. . . .

Because the sixth-grader-to-be hasn't as much as a shoulder on his right side, the possibility of developing an artificial limb to help him out seems remote. What's that do to his future as a Lyons Lion?

"Wouldn't you say that at least fifty percent of an athlete's success is desire? Ronny has more desire than any person, child or adult, I've known. He plays basketball as well as he does baseball, and he's already talking about being a center or tight end in football. I don't think there's any doubt he'll be a star in every sport," Mathers said.

Keep your eyes on this kid.

December 20, 1981[4]

[Before you read this column you need to know that the varsity basketball coach at Lyons, Greg Kamp—a good friend of the Gustafson family—said through the years that although Ron might be able to play elementary and junior high basketball, he'd never play for him on the Lyons varsity team.]

Kamp, too, has been both amazed and proud of Gustafson's success in overcoming adversity.

"He doesn't ask for any special treatment and he doesn't get any," says Kamp. "He's always positive. I don't think he ever thought he couldn't play. I know there are times when I forget he's got only one arm. Sometimes I'll tell the guys they've got to dribble with both hands and Ron will joke with me and say, 'But Coach, I can't do that.'"

Realistically, it may be the *only* endeavor impossible in Ron Gustafson's eyes.

February 4, 1982[5]

Over the years, I've seen some incredible moments of courage on the athletic field. I've seen kids play with a lot of heart. I've seen kids use the springboard of athletics to overcome some pretty big odds. I've seen guts, raw desire and talent maximized to the "nth" degree. But I have never in my life seen a more wonderful, more awe-inspiring moment in sports than when Lyons' Ron Gustafson took the basketball court against Oakland-Craig last Friday. . . .

Ron Gustafson is only a sophomore this year. He's not only a starter but also quite possibly the best basketball player on the Lyons team. With an extraordinary amount of self-discipline, positive thinking, dedication, work!-work!-work! and, yes, pain—the kind that you and I will never know in our lifetime—Ron made himself an ATHLETE. Not merely an athlete. An outstanding athlete. . . .

Young Mr. Gustafson dribbles behind his back. He can shoot with the best of them from twenty feet out. He can mix it up and rebound with the big boys. There are, perhaps, tougher defensive players than Ron—but not many. And I have NEVER seen a high school kid rifle passes and assists the way he does. I can think of one who comes close: his all-class, all-state brother Jim, catalyst on that unbeaten Lyons team of 1979, the best high school player I have ever seen.

And Ron's only a sophomore. Heaven only knows how great this kid could become if he had two arms and two legs like the rest of us. But Ron doesn't dwell on what might have been. He dwells, instead, passionately, on what can be.

Ron Gustafson, ladies and gentlemen, is the living end. And thank goodness we'll get to watch him, and learn from him, another couple years yet.

August 24, 1996[6]

Former Lyons athlete Ron Gustafson will be the first recipient of an award the Nebraska High School Sports Hall of Fame has named for him.

The Gustafson Inspiration Award is intended to honor people who have achieved success in high school athletics while overcoming monumental obstacles. As a youth in 1975, Gustafson was hurt in a farm accident that cut off his right arm and mangled his right leg. He came back to be a high school basketball player and left-handed pitcher.

Not only did Ron play high school sports, he started three years in basketball, ran track, and played baseball and one year of football. He also was a member of the Future Farmers of America and band, and was *elected president of his sophomore class. And he even got a shot at college ball. After beating the player favored to win the one-on-one tournament at a high school basketball camp—a young man who just happened to be the son of the basketball coach at Kearney State College—Ron was invited to walk on at Kearney. He made the team, but after blowing out his knee two years in a row, his athletic career was finally over.*

Ron is now the president and founder of Integrity Systems, Inc., in Omaha, Nebraska, and is a frequent inspirational speaker at school assemblies, churches, and business functions. Today he tells audiences there are two main ingredients in turning a setback into a comeback:

1. Never give up;

2. Always look for the next challenge; don't settle for where you're at.

Ron continues to live by those principles and therefore is still turning setbacks into comebacks.

Notes

1. "Six Week Hospital Stay Over—Ronny is Home," *Lyons Mirror-Sun*, October 23, 1975, 1.

2. "Jumble by Jim," *Lyons Mirror-Sun*, October 23, 1975, 2.

3. Dewaine Gahan, "Gahan's Game Plan: A remarkable young man," *Fremont Tribune*, August 9, 1977, 10.

4. Steve Allspach, "Siouxland sportlight: Lyons' Ron Gustafson asks no favors," *The Sioux City Journal*, December 20, 1981, C7.

5. Dewaine Gahan, "The Hot Corner ... as I see it: Talk About Inspiration!" *Fremont Tribune*, February 4, 1982, 9.

6. Stu Pospisil, "Hall of Fame to Honor Ex-Lyons Athlete," *Omaha World-Herald*, August 24, 1996.

3

WHEN DEATH DOESN'T
TAKE A HOLIDAY

Sometimes you don't have to look very far to find men and women of courage, although you have to keep a sharp lookout to spot them. These folks aren't likely to walk up and announce themselves as heroes. In fact, most prefer backstage to center stage. But by their consistent, faithful behavior in the midst of dreadful circumstances, they earn the honors they so often shun.

In our view, Pam Brigman is one of these courageous individuals who truly deserves the name hero. She would deny it, of course, but she really is a person of deep faith and consistent bravery—we've observed her unselfish and giving nature for too long to agree with her own humble self-assessment. We've watched her work with distraught people who contact the Outreach of Hope for help and encouragement, and we've been amazed at her ability to keep giving out of her deep reservoirs of compassion, understanding, and love. And we've also watched as tragedy after tragedy struck her own family—and yet she kept moving ahead. "I do not see myself as a woman who has been courageous," Pam protests, "I am no hero." But read her story for yourself and make your own judgment.

Death is never easy to face, especially when it's the death of a loved one. But when death starts ganging up on you and seems to take grisly pleasure in snatching your dear ones from you, rapid-fire before you can take a breath—

One ...

Two ...

Three ...

Four!

—then what can you do? If you're Pam Brigman, you simply continue doing what you've always done. Because in your weary eyes, there's simply no choice.

"I have observed more death in the last few years than I ever thought possible," Pam declares. And yet she keeps moving forward. She also asks questions, hard questions we often don't like to hear. "Why do we try to fool ourselves by pretending that struggle and death will somehow avoid us?" she wonders. "Then, when it does look us straight in the eye, we are so surprised. And if we do manage to overcome, others assume we have great storehouses of strength that enable us to survive such disasters. Too often, I have been told, 'You have such courage.' Try as I may, I cannot convince people that this is not a matter of courage. It is a fact of nature that we must all endure the ugly face of death."

Round One of Pam's personal odyssey of grief began when she helped her mother through the last stages of terminal cancer. "I was raised to care for her without question until the bitter end," she says. "Courage was not an issue. It was a matter of accepting the fact that no one else was able to help."

Pam moved her frail mother into her own house, took care of her many needs, and administered morphine when the pain grew unbearable. Her mom hung on to life until her body could no longer function; then Pam took care of all the funeral arrangements. "These were my gifts, given out of love and loyalty, to the woman who raised me," Pam says. "Life was precious to my mom, and she still is precious to me. I miss her friendship, her laugh, and her loyalty."

Round Two occurred just six months later when Pam's husband, Mike—only forty-seven years old—suffered a series of debilitating strokes. Now he, too, could no longer function on his own. And Pam was faced with another choice: should the man she loved be placed in a nursing home or other care facility? But really, there was no choice at all; Pam could not and would not renege on her pledge given some twenty-five years before to bind herself to this man, for better or worse, "'til death do us part." No, she would take care of her husband, even though he had been categorized as one hundred percent disabled.

"Suddenly I was faced with another opportunity to give to someone I loved," Pam explains. "I knew I wanted to care for him at home. In my own strength I had nothing left to give. But God tells us, 'In your weakness I am strong.' I depended on his strength to help me keep my promise, and he *never* failed me."

When her husband grew ill, it became clear to Pam why the Lord had allowed her to experience the hardship and pain of her mother's death. In all his wisdom, he was preparing her for the worst experience of her life. "It was a matter of acceptance," she says simply.

After four hard months of rehabilitation, Pam's husband slowly began to improve and even managed to get up and walk a few tiny steps. He could not talk, use his right arm, read, or see out of one eye, but Pam loved him with all her heart. "I would rather have been married to him in a wheelchair than to anyone else I knew," she says.

And yet he died.

"It was difficult to imagine life without Mike," Pam admits. "How could I go on in this world, how could I pick out his casket, how could I raise our eleven-year-old daughter alone or tell her that she would never again see her dad alive? And how could I sleep in the bed where he had died? How could I live without the man with whom I had shared everything for a quarter of a century?

"Simple—I had no choice. It was a matter of acceptance. It was not courage that saw me through, but God's grace and my faith in him. Endurance is one of God's greatest gifts."

Pam holds on to God's words in Isaiah: "Remember no more the reproach of your widowhood. For your Maker is your husband—the LORD Almighty is his name—the Holy One of Israel is your Redeemer" (Isaiah

54:4–5). And she claims this psalm of David: "A father to the fatherless, a defender of widows, is God in his holy dwelling" (Psalm 68:5).

Just one day after her husband's funeral, the bell for Round Three tolled. Pam's stepmother, Marie, was killed instantly when a vehicle blind-sided her as she was making her way to the hospital to see Pam's terminally ill father.

Pam had come to dearly love this woman who "could make anything." For the twenty-two years Marie was married to Pam's dad, she crocheted a vast collection of dolls and crafts—a collection that on her death went to Pam's kids, since this generous woman never had children of her own.

With Marie's untimely death Pam was faced with yet another choice. Just one day after Mike's funeral, should she leave her daughter in the care of her older sister in order to bury her stepmother in far away Indiana? Or should she let her aged and hospitalized father agonize over the funeral arrangements by himself? Again, there seemed no real choice. How could she force her terminally ill father, a man unable to leave the hospital, to be responsible for a final act of love for his spouse? She left for Indiana.

Pam loved her father and on her way to visit him reminisced over the good times they had enjoyed. "Dad was always fun at games, but the truth is, he cheated," Pam said. "My children knew it; we all knew it. If you wanted Dad to play, he just had to win."

But not even her father could cheat death. "The day of my stepmother's funeral, the hospital was ready to discharge Dad to a hospice facility," Pam said. "They could do no more for him there. I didn't want to leave him alone in a strange place, yet he was too weak to travel back to Colorado with me, where my youngest daughter needed me at home. God's timing is remarkable. The morning after my stepmother's funeral, my father went home to be with the Lord."

Round Four had sounded. Yet another funeral, yet another loved one gone. And yet Pam felt a puff of divine grace in the whirlwind of her personal grief. "Through it all I experienced God's enduring strength," she declared.

Pam's elder daughter, Lisa Harding, says that "the incredible part of Mom's tale is that, to speak to her, she hasn't done anything special. In her darkest hours, she reminds herself of others who have suffered through harder tragedies and lived. She reminds herself of all of her blessings without putting others down. She is truly a daughter of our Lord and a heroine to everyone she touches. Her courage to set herself aside to help others is a gift from God."

Of course, people of courage don't "feel" any less than others do. In some ways, they feel more deeply than the rest of us because they enter into life more thoroughly. That is certainly true of Pam. "I loved my parents, my husband, and my life the way I knew it," she says. "My family was so important to me, and losing them all in such an abrupt manner still fills my heart with pain. I struggle with grief, with knowing my husband will never see his daughter graduate, get married, or have children. He will never see her successes or hug her during her failures. I will always miss my dream of growing old with this man and the fellowship and conflicts of a good marriage. I will always miss being the daughter of my parents and picking up the phone just to shoot the breeze."

And yet ... if you were to ask Pam if she would choose to go back, she would answer with a firm "No!" She has grown so much personally and in deep reserves of faith that she would never choose to go back. "God has taught me so much, changed me, loved and protected me, as only he can," she says. "Praise God, I never have to endure the loss of him."

Pam continues to work diligently with the hurting people who seek encouragement from the Outreach of Hope. Even though she still struggles with legal hassles over the sale of the family business. Even though she has been suffering for over a year with constant pain from an ankle broken several times. Even though now she is the sole breadwinner for a house whose upkeep is anything but easy. She keeps plowing ahead—and I call that courage.

Pam doesn't think she's courageous because, as she says, "fear is something that never left my side, fear of so many things like death, loneliness and the unknown." In her mind, only one person is truly worthy of the term "courageous."

"Only one man went to the cross and died willingly for others," she says. "He had a choice, and in my eyes, only Jesus Christ deserves the title of courageous. Because of his courage, I am saved and will one day see again in heaven all those I have loved and lost. If not for the courageous act of our Lord, I would have to endure suffering and death without love, without hope, and most importantly, without him! I trust him at his word: 'For I know the plans I have for you,' declares the LORD, 'plans to prosper you and not to harm you, plans to give you hope and a future' (Jeremiah 29:11)."

4

"TOGETHER COURAGE"— THE BEST KIND OF ALL

It's not often that the Outreach of Hope receives two independent refer-rals for the same person the same week, but that's what happened for one special little boy from Cedarville, Ohio. When it became known that Andrew Johnson, then nine years old, would lose his leg because of a can-cerous tumor, two women—one a nurse, the other a school guidance counselor—called to ask us to contact Andrew's parents. When we did reach his family, we found not one but several heroes. All of the family members are helping each other to find courage—and I think "together courage" is the best kind of all.

Have you ever felt as though you were attracting trouble like yellow jackets to a picnic? The last few years, Bob and Debbie Johnson must have felt exactly like that. Around every bend, it seemed, trouble was lying in wait.

In 1994 Bob was diagnosed with an aggressive melanoma. The couple has five children—then ages seventeen, fifteen, eleven, six, and four—and Debbie confessed to lying awake at night and asking herself strange questions such as, "Who will walk our daughter down the aisle?" Through aggressive medical treatment and a potent faith in God, Bob appears to have beaten the disease and now has been cancer free for four years.

But that was just the first assault.

On April 29, 1996, brothers Joshua and Andrew were playing on the Johnson's living room floor. When Andrew took one last leap over his older brother, he crashed to the floor and injured his knee. Mom had seen this kind of accident before and immediately iced the painful leg, but the next day the injury felt no better and Andrew still couldn't walk. A trip to the hospital for X-rays revealed a break—and a mass initially diagnosed as a benign tumor. Doctors said Andrew needed surgery for the leg and would spend eight weeks in a cast.

While the family waited at the hospital on a rainy afternoon to return home—that night was Aime's senior prom—Debbie saw the doctor running into the building. In moments he was at their door. He motioned her out to the hall and quietly reported that the tumor was "unusual" and was being sent for analysis to Sloan Kettering Memorial Hospital in New York. They would know the results of the tests in a few days.

Debbie and her son went home, but she couldn't banish the cold fear that clutched at her throat. "Each time the phone rang I felt sick," she said. "The phone became my enemy." Four days later Debbie and Bob were called to the doctor's office; while they learned the results of the tests, Andrew sat alone in another room. The doctor confirmed the couple's worst fears, first of cancer and then of amputation. At this Debbie's knees buckled and Bob gently lifted her back to a standing position. It was May 15, 1996, and their nine-year-old had been diagnosed with osteogenic sarcoma, a form of bone cancer.

As Andrew underwent more tests, Bob and Debbie huddled alone in a secluded doorway, feeling empty, brokenhearted, and helpless. Although he was as worried as his wife, Bob reassured Debbie, "We have to have hope. The worry will destroy us, but hope and prayer can get us all through it."

Cancer treatment proceeds rapidly for children and Andrew left immediately for the hospital, where his oncology team was waiting. He was scheduled for surgery to implant a port[1] in his chest for administering his chemo treatments while his parents were handed a large notebook prepared for cancer patients. Then they were briefed on Andrew's "protocol"—the drugs he would take, their effects, his diet, etc. They learned their son would undergo ten chemo treatments lasting three months, followed by the amputation, followed by thirty-six more weeks of chemo. They also heard they could change their minds about possible treatments at any time—the choice was theirs alone.

*A*nd thus began a new and agonizing chapter in the life of the Johnson family. For the next ten months, Debbie and Andrew would spend an average of twenty to twenty-five days each month in the hospital. The amputation was scheduled for August 12—but as the fateful day approached, neither Debbie nor Bob could bring themselves to tell their active little boy he was about to lose his leg. Finally, the day came when they had to break the terrible news.

"We had a nice family dinner and planned to go to a miniature golf course later," Debbie said. "During dinner I prayed for God's guidance, assurance, even a reprieve. While we were eating Andrew announced that all he wanted to do the next summer was play baseball—and that was our gift from God. We knew he could play ball with a prosthetic leg."

Mother, father, and son sat quietly after taking the last bite of their meal. Bob recalls, "It was the hardest thing I've ever done, keeping strong on the outside (for Andrew), yet dying on the inside." Bob gently told Andrew of the amputation, emphasizing the "why" of it all. The cancer had destroyed the growth plate and Andrew's leg would not grow properly. If surgeons tried to "repair" it there would be many surgeries to lengthen the leg and he would not be able to run, jump, and play sports. This route also made the cancer more likely to return and Andrew quickly said, "I don't want that." Already he had suffered through five surgeries and he didn't want any more. He wanted to play baseball. Then it was time to tell him of the last surgery, the amputation—it would be tougher, but he would be able to play and run using an artificial leg.

"Andrew cried, we cried, we all rocked and cried and reassured Andrew," Debbie recalls. "It wasn't easy, those final moments, but Andrew understood it all and fell into my arms for comfort."

Within days of this conversation Andrew's leg was amputated. Meanwhile, life went on for the rest of the family. Aaron, the oldest son and then a sophomore in college, turned his talents to help run the family's home-based business, an art company. Eldest daughter Aime graduated from high school, turned eighteen, and became engaged the same week. Joshua, an eighth grader, "seemed lost" amidst the chaos. And the youngest, Natalie, was being cared for by a host of family and friends. "There were many days I cried for her," Debbie said of her "baby," "because I did not know at that moment who had her." Nattie's anger eventually bubbled up out of her feisty eight-year-old soul. She was tired of her mother's absence, tired of Andrew's illness. She felt left out by all the attention lavished on her brother and one day asked her mother if she could have her "pinkie" amputated. The hospital psychologist told Bob and Debbie this was typical of siblings lost in the disruption of cancer treatment. Everyone involved was made aware of Nattie's needs.

One day while still in the hospital, Andrew received a special package from the Outreach of Hope. We included a video chronicling my own battle with cancer and subsequent amputation, and Andrew absorbed every word. Debbie even described it as "a turning point of hope and renewal and interest in Andrew's life." Andrew received another boost when he turned on the TV and saw exciting scenes from the para-olympic games, featuring amputees and other athletes with disabilities. Bob and Debbie saw it as another gift from God.

After his amputation Andrew received a two-week reprieve from chemotherapy. Then it was back to the fearsome drugs. While the other Johnson kids returned to school, and Bob ran at full speed with the kids, the business, and daily thirty-mile trips to see his wife and son, Andrew and Debbie returned to the hospital—a regimen they would endure for nearly a year.

Not all was focused on battling cancer, however. Through all the hospital visits and trials of chemotherapy, a wedding had to be planned. Aime decided she wanted to marry while still in college and set the wedding date for a week after Thanksgiving.

She picked a beautiful day and five hundred guests attended the ceremony to help share the family's joy. Witnesses also took in a minor miracle—Andrew's first steps after his amputation. "The little scamp surprised us," Debbie explained. "Before Bob and Aime entered the sanctuary, Bob wheeled Andrew, the ring-bearer, to the entrance. Andrew stood up out of his wheelchair. His dad asked, 'Are you sure?' Andrew nodded his head, got out of his wheelchair, and walked down the aisle. And everyone cried—tears of joy this time."

As she looks back at that day, Debbie considers the wedding "a wonderful gift and distraction. But to fit joy into all of this sadness can be very difficult." Her mind drifts back to the time a week before the wedding when she left the hospital to make Thanksgiving dinner. She flipped on the radio and heard Pam Thum's song, "Life Is Hard But God Is Good" and thought, *My life is being played on the radio!* That week, four children being treated for cancer at Andrew's hospital died within three days of each other.

"All I wanted to do was escape," Debbie says. "The death of a child is incomprehensible. When a child dies with cancer, you hear the little one cry and cry. Their pain medicine is increased, increased. And eventually you no longer hear the cries of the child—now the parents cry. Those were long nights, haunting nights, life-changing nights. I heard sounds that do not go away. I remembered the halls of the hospital being filled with voices singing 'Jesus Loves the Little Children.' Now, only quiet tears were left."

March was a much better month. Andrew finished his in-hospital chemo. From then on it would be outpatient chemo until May 1—his last day of the stuff! On March 13 I met the Johnson family after I spoke in Pleasant Hill, Ohio, near their home. Andrew seemed so excited; two months before he had called to announce he was to receive a Young Hero Award on February 15. I spent time with him that night and told him to call us anytime.

And March just kept getting better. Bob signed up Andrew for Little League and wheeled him in to his first meeting—a bald, frail, one-legged ball player. Debbie wonders what his coach must have thought. She didn't have to wonder how he would react, however. "Coach Atley was incredible," she raves. "Two weeks into practice, Andrew received his new leg at practice. Bob would carry Andrew from place to place on the field because our son was too weak to do much. What an amazing sight! Andrew gained strength rapidly from the workout. Coach Atley played Andrew *every game* at third base. But all Andrew wanted to do was pitch. The last game of the season he got his wish; he pitched two innings and got a few strikes! He also 'ran' to home plate for a run." All this, just ten months after his amputation.

About this time Andrew started going through a major grieving process. "Why me?" he would ask. "Why aren't there other kids like me?" He returned to school half days, but because of his amputation he didn't really want to be there. But by May his strength was returning and he again started becoming active. He attended a Boy Scout camp and continued to play baseball. Andrew wanted to meet another young amputee . It turned out someone needed to meet Andrew, too. Six-year-old amputee Phillip Bishop watches everything Andrew does—run, ride a bike—and he loves his nine-year-old hero. Andrew has given his young friend hope.

And speaking of hope—Andrew's kid sister Natalie had a question for her mom not too long ago. "When will Andrew's leg grow back?" she wondered.

"That's what heaven's for, Nattie!" her mom replied. "Life goes on—and God is good!"

Even when it seems as if neither is true.

Andrew broke his stump leg on August 18, 1997, two and a half inches above where his knee had been. He was playing dodgeball at the time. "What a boy!" his mom says. The mishap is a mental setback— Andrew wanted to start school standing but had to settle for a wheel-

chair—but you can't keep a dodgeball-playing boy down for long. In fact, Andrew's last prosthesis was so worn out from his athletic activities that his mom says at the end it was held together with "gum and staples." What a boy, indeed.

Notes

1. A port is a semi-permanent opening, something like an IV, that allows medicine to be introduced into the body.

5

FINISHING THE RACE

When Melanie Cooper was seven years old, she slipped on a patch of ice in her backyard and hurt her arm. X-rays showed no break—but in time, further tests revealed that the ulna bone in her forearm was growing faster than the radius bone, causing discomfort and pain. A necessary operation was postponed until Melanie's arm had stopped growing.

In 1990 when Melanie was a freshman in high school, doctors removed a small piece of her ulna to shorten it; after a short time of healing the bone began to dissolve. A subsequent bone graft ended in the same result and by the next year her radius also appeared to be dissolving—and a large lump had appeared on her forearm. Surgeons believed the lump was caused by an allergic reaction to the metal plate in her arm. Melanie was referred to a specialist in Detroit; there she learned she had a desmoid tumor, the same kind of slow-growing but tenacious cancer that ended my baseball career. Melanie knew all about tumors. Her little brother and grandfather had both died from a type of brain tumor called a glioblastoma.

In November 1991 Melanie had surgery to remove the desmoid. A segment of her ulna from the wrist to the middle of her forearm also was removed, and her radius bone was "scooped out" where the tumor had destroyed it. Seven weeks of radiation followed. At the end of the treatments her weakened arm broke, requiring reconstructive surgery at the Mayo Clinic. The desmoid reappeared after her first year of college in 1994, this time in her elbow, and Melanie began two years of chemotherapy treatments.

I first met Melanie when I gave my testimony in Grand Rapids, Michigan. After my talk this college sophomore wanted me to autograph my book, *When You Can't Come Back*. She approached me, handed me her book, and explained, "I'm also fighting a desmoid tumor." I asked her a few questions, then gave her my office number and asked her to call me.

The next March I visited Calvin College to share my testimony. Melanie's college chaplain asked her to coordinate the event and serve as my escort. She sat next to me at a student luncheon and during the course of the meal I leaned over and said, "Melanie, tell me what the doctors say about your arm."

"Well, I'm on chemotherapy," she reminded me.

"Yes, I know that," I replied, "but what if the chemo doesn't work?"

She had tried to push that thought out of her head but hesitantly answered, "There is the possibility of amputation."

"And how does that rest on your heart, Melanie?"

"Oh, I would hate it," she said vigorously. I knew that feeling well! Yet I responded, "Don't stop fighting, but don't let that fight get in the way of any special plans God may have for you."

The weekend after my Calvin visit Melanie was in a lot of pain following a chemo treatment. When her boyfriend, Brian, dropped her off at her dorm, tears streamed down her cheeks. Brian reached over to wipe them away and gently asked, "Melanie, what if you just let go of your arm?" She quickly jumped on his remark, explaining how she couldn't be a whole person with just one arm. She spit out a long list why—from washing dishes in the sink to doing her hair—and her tears fell along with unreasonable words.

When she was done, Brian lifted her chin and whispered, "Melanie, your life would change, but you would still have your heart and that's the most important part of who you are." Throughout her ordeal, Brian would repeat this heartfelt counsel—that no matter what happened to her arm, Melanie would still be the same person inside. It brought untold comfort to a soul in frequent turmoil.

In June, after a year of treatments, doctors gave Melanie a two-week respite from chemo—so Melanie, her parents, and Brian took off across the country to Montana. "I was grouchy and weary from chemo and college exams," she said. "It rained almost every day of our vacation, but we hiked on the muddy mountain trails anyway. One day the sun came out and Brian and I decided to hike to the top of Scenic Point. It was a tough hike, over rocky ledges and countless switchbacks, and I often wanted to give up and turn around. But Brian would reach back, take my hand, and help me take the next step forward."

When the couple at last made it to the summit, a glorious view of the mountains took their breath away. Melanie realized that climbing the mountain was just like trying to tackle her personal trial—but once on the top, the view was tremendous. What a thrill to see how far she'd already come!

In July Melanie returned to her summer job at Amway. Several times people told her she "just had to meet Julie," the new receptionist who had lost her right arm to cancer when she was eight years old.

"I was frightened to meet Julie, but when at last I walked into the lobby and saw her, I noticed something different," Melanie said. "She simply shined! It had to be her brilliant smile."

Julie and Melanie became good friends and told each other their personal stories. They both battled tumors in their dominant right arm and underwent chemo, and both believed their experiences had shaped them into what God wanted them to be.

In early September Melanie started the nursing program at Calvin. On the first day she discovered that Betsy, the young woman who sat next to her the previous semester in microbiology, had been assigned to her clinical group. Brian and Melanie had become engaged that summer, and about the same time Betsy also had agreed to marry a young man from Reformed Bible College—the same school Brian attended. Betsy and Melanie discovered they shared similar tastes in music and in many other areas.

The pair soon committed to running with each other every day. On their first run, Melanie could barely finish a two-mile jog. But every morning Betsy encouraged her friend that she could do it. One day they ran all the way around Reeds Lake—six miles. Flush with excitement, they signed up for their first 10K (6.2 miles) and began to train for it. But a week before the race Betsy had to back out.

The day of the race Melanie woke up to blizzard-like conditions, but she wanted to run the race anyway. It was too cold for spectators and the starting line was covered with snow, yet the runners all took off when the gun sounded.

"I remember where I realized the race would be difficult," Melanie said. "I rounded a corner onto another road and met a bone-chilling wind. My long hair formed into what felt like icicles, and my cheeks became numb from the icy snow sticking to them. The visibility was poor and I squinted into the distance for the flashing light that would indicate the next corner. I was tired at the halfway point as I heard two girls with stopwatches shout my time. I realized the course to come would be tougher, but I believed I could do it."

The last mile of the race called for more endurance than Melanie had ever needed. Officials who had been stationed at the mile marks were slowly passing her in cars. An ambulance crept by. Melanie then caught sight of a rescue truck at her heels, its four-way flashers on. *I'm the last runner!* she realized—and her spirits sank. Feeling totally alone, she started talking to God. "Please, God, please don't leave me . . . ." Yet she heard nothing in reply and wondered where he was.

Suddenly, through the blinding snow, Melanie saw two people at the next corner. She was almost finished! One young man approached her with a big smile and said, "That can't be Melanie Cooper running the 10K of her life . . . It *is* you!" The man was a fellow runner who had crossed the finish line long before. Melanie kept running, but also began to sob.

"It wasn't so much the fact that I was tired and cold as it was that God had heard my cries and sent this person to encourage me," she said. The runner told her she was almost done. "This is so hard," she replied. "I know," he said, and picked up his pace to run beside her. "This part is a little tough, but you've already come six miles. Do you see that person ahead, all bundled up in blankets? As soon as you round that corner, you're going to feel like Superman with the wind at your back. You're going to fly right through the finish line!"

He was right. Melanie did cross the finish line and she did feel like Superman. About five people stood waiting in the blowing snow, lingering just for her. They hadn't given up on her. Melanie wept when she finished the race.

When the icicles melted and she finally warmed, Melanie reflected on the race and how it seemed to parallel her life. She was able to see God working through the people and events he brought into her life just when she thought she couldn't take another step.

It was a needed lesson, because within the next month Melanie made another visit to the DeVos Children's Hem/Onc Clinic. Her doctor felt her arm with gentle strokes and Melanie reported she was having increasing pain. The doctor carefully told her she favored stronger chemo in an effort to reduce the troublesome lump in her arm. Through tears, Melanie replied she would make her decision after Christmas. She didn't want to choose stronger chemo; she was tired of the regimen and it might force a disruption in her college schedule. Melanie also consulted with her other doctor in Detroit, who said that if she chose, they could bring an end to the struggle by amputating her arm. She wasn't happy with the choice.

Since desmoid tumors grow slowly, Melanie had some time to decide. Finally she decided to go on aggressive chemo and continue as a full-time nursing student.

I called Melanie out of the blue on January 16, the day she received her first aggressive chemo treatment. I hadn't heard from her in awhile and just wanted to know how she was doing. I didn't know of her decision to pursue such aggressive treatment. Melanie told me she considered that phone call too great to be mere coincidence; she saw it as a gift from God. "You and Jan seem to come into my life during the toughest days to encourage me in my faith," she told me, "and that is a miracle."

In my eyes, Melanie is the real miracle. By July 1996 at her six month checkup, it appeared the aggressive chemotherapy had done its work. Doctors could find no tumor in her arm and talk of amputation was firmly placed on a shelf.

On May 10, 1997, Melanie received her nursing pin, signifying that she had earned her nursing degree from Calvin College. She began working as a nurse at DeVos Children's Hospital. And on June 7, 1997, Melanie Cooper became Melanie Newhouse when she married Brian, her high school sweetheart and unswerving encourager who stood by her since she was first diagnosed.

There is still concern for her arm—she suffers from pain and is unable to bend her elbow—and she must report for a checkup every two months. Meanwhile, Melanie continues to live to the fullest and witnesses little miracles every day.

6

CIRCUMSTANCES DON'T LAST FOREVER (BUT GOD DOES)

Joshua Sundquist was a healthy eight-year-old when he first noticed persistent pain in his left leg. Many tests, countless anxious moments, and one year later, doctors amputated his leg so that the tumor growing there would spread no further. His amputation occurred in the summer of 1994, but it hardly seems to slow him down. This thirteen-year-old has a lot we should listen to. Here's what Joshua says:

"Daddy, how many people do you think get cancer?" I asked one day when I was seven years old. "Probably one out of ten sometime in their lives," he answered. I thought that was a lot, but I was confident that nothing like that could ever happen to me.

Now I know cancer can happen to anyone, whether it's a family member, a friend, or even you.

When I was eight I started having pains in my left leg. For awhile we thought they were just growing pains, but when they got worse, I went to the doctor. I had several tests and two biopsies before I was diagnosed. I was nine when I woke up from the second biopsy to hear my parents tell me, "Joshua, you have a fast-growing kind of bone cancer called Ewing's Sarcoma."

Instantly my mind said, *Cancer? **Wham!** You're dead.*

My parents quickly explained that not everyone dies from cancer and that doctors have new ways of treating it. I immediately started chemotherapy, which kills fast growing cells like cancer. But hair cells are also fast-growing, which is why most people lose their hair when being treated for cancer. When I started to lose my hair, my friends and kids from church showed how much they cared about me. Twenty kids came over to my house to get a "chemo cut," as one of the makeshift barbers called everyone's crew cuts.

After three chemo treatments, my tumor had not grown, but it was not getting any smaller, either. My family faced the decision of whether to amputate my leg. After praying a lot, we decided that amputation would be the best choice. That was *very* hard, because I wasn't sure how my friends would treat me. I also didn't know whether I would be able to participate in any sports, which I loved.

After my amputation I was supposed to recover in the hospital for three weeks. But after three days I was running laps on my crutches around the children's floor of the UVA hospital. They released me after five days.

That was July of 1995, and I still had fifteen chemotherapy treatments left. I went back and forth between three-day and five-day hospital stays. Normally I was home for two weeks between each treatment. The first week I would feel pretty lousy and not be very hungry. The second week I started to get better, but then I had to go back to the hospital when my body was able to go through another chemotherapy cycle. I had to get shots to make my body ready for more chemotherapy. At first the doctors said my mom or dad might have to give me the shot—or else I would have to do it myself. All of those options sounded terrible to me. But God provided a nurse in our church, Kaye, who was willing to come over to my house every day and inject the medicine.

I was never very hungry while in the hospital. I was glad they had new nausea drugs and although I didn't throw up much, I just wasn't hungry. I also had to urinate a lot because they were pumping tons of fluids into my body to get the chemotherapy medicine through my system as quickly as possible. I was very tired and laid in bed most of the time.

For the first few days of my hospital stays, I was able to do several things. They had a classroom where I could play the computer and use CD-ROMs. They also had a TV show that they broadcasted every couple of days to all the rooms. Patients could be on the program if they wanted to, or they could stay in their rooms and watch. If it was a day where they were doing a game show, like bingo, we could play from our rooms and win prizes.

God was with me through everything. I especially thought about several of my favorite verses. Joshua 1:9 says not to fear because we can know that God is with us and he is Lord. This means that wherever we are, whatever we're doing and whenever it is, God will be with us. That's why we don't need to be afraid.

Another good verse is also about fear. Psalm 56:3 says, "When I am afraid, I will trust in God." This is one of the first verses I ever memorized. I learned it to help me not to be afraid of the dark.

My last verse is Romans 8:28—"And we know that God causes all things to work together for good to those who love God; to those who are called according to His purpose" (NASB). I think that many times when someone is having a hard time, people just recite this verse and say, "See, God says that this major disaster in your life is good. So be happy. Bye." That's just not the way it works. A lot of times bad things happen that just seem bad for the rest of our lives, and we don't know why God let them happen. But that doesn't mean those things can't help others or strengthen your own faith. They will always glorify God in the end, whether we see how or not. I am reminded of the song, "Don't worry, be happy." That's good advice, but it's really not quite as simple as that.

I am thirteen now and have been off chemotherapy treatment for two years. Many people have been praying for me and the elders of my church anointed me in a special prayer service. My hair has come back! And I am always hungry (or at least it seems that way).

I have also participated in a lot of sports. I learned to ride my bike with one leg, so I bought a bike and started mountain biking. A few months ago I completed a fifty mile bike ride. I have learned to ski on one leg and recently took part in a race for disabled skiers. I had the fastest time of any one! It is possible that I might be on a local ski team next year. I also enjoy swimming, running, golf, playing soccer, riding horses, and jumping on our backyard trampoline.

Last spring I went to Florida to help raise money for children's hospitals with the Children's Miracle Network telethon. I was on TV with Steve Young, the star quarterback of the San Francisco 49ers. I also got to meet President Bill and Hillary Clinton at the White House.

As you can see, God has blessed me very much. He has helped me to overcome and persevere through my problems. He will do the same for you if you trust him and remember that circumstances don't last forever. But God does.

By August of 1995 Joshua was doing "great," according to his parents, and was asked to speak at a local gathering of the Fellowship of Christian Athletes. His speech went so well that many others have since invited him to address their groups.

After being tested every three months for one year, Joshua was officially pronounced in remission. Yet Joshua knows that cancer is a killer—at least five children from the hospital that treated Joshua had died by the beginning of 1996. And in May of that year a CT scan revealed spots on Joshua's lungs measuring two to three millimeters in size. If another scan six weeks later showed they had grown, Joshua would have to undergo more chemotherapy. A month and a half later the family was relieved to hear that the spots had not grown—and Joshua and his parents held out hope that they never would.

Like any of us, Joshua worried that the cancer might return, but despite his anxiety he attended three camps that summer (one a cancer camp) and also discovered the brave new world of the Internet. Some of his favorite hobbies are playing drums, speaking about hard times, and working on his own website. In the summer of 1997 he learned to play volleyball and also spoke at a local church on "Getting Through Hard Times."

Joshua and his family continue to give out books supplied by the Outreach of Hope to people battling cancer. Today's Heroes *is one of his favorites. He now goes in for checkups every six months and continues to enjoy a very active lifestyle—just like any other energetic thirteen-year-old. He and his family monitor his condition closely, but that careful scrutiny never replaces or diminishes Joshua's firm trust in God. He continues to remind whoever will listen that "circumstances don't last forever, but God does." He's one great kid and one powerful evangelist—and he's not letting cancer or amputation stand in the way of his trust in God for everything life has to offer. That's why he's my hero.*

7

WHAT MATTERS MOST?

In mid-July 1995, Jay Snyder was diagnosed with colon cancer and he and his wife, Diana, began struggling with the many overwhelming issues that confront a family battling a life-threatening disease. In many ways, the struggle was hardest on Diana—and Jay did what he could to reassure her that she'd be OK, no matter what happened to him. He had reason for such confidence, because in several ways both Jay and Diana had been prepared for the crisis now facing them.

Finding the strength to live is crucial for a patient battling cancer, but it's just as critical for the patient's spouse—and that's often the harder task. In the case of Jay and Diana Snyder, the Lord made the challenge easier by placing just the right people in their lives. He also had prepared them in many ways for the difficult days ahead.

"In the early 1980s," Jay explained, "I experienced what Diana is now going through. At that time she was critically ill and I had to face the grim reality that she might never return to health. Thank God she did, but it took four long years to happen."

Jay's own battle for life began on the evening of June 14, 1995, when the intermittent abdominal pain he had attributed to stress suddenly intensified. "At 7:00 P.M., I was afraid I was going to die," Jay said. "By 11:00 P.M., I was afraid I wasn't!"

The next morning he visited the Mayo Clinic near his home in Scottsdale, Arizona. His doctor initially thought Jay suffered from diverticulitis and was about to send him home with antibiotics, but by the end of the examination Jay was on his way to the hospital for more tests. For two days doctors tried to identify the problem; on Friday evening a surgeon walked into Jay's room and told him he needed surgery that very night. Medication had reduced his pain and Jay suggested they wait until morning. "You don't understand," the surgeon replied. "You have a complete blockage, and we suspect cancer. If we wait until morning, there is a chance of a perforation of the colon, and if that occurs, your life could be in immediate danger."

The surgery went ahead as recommended and the next morning Jay's doctor confirmed his diagnosis: cancer. Still, the doctor thought they had removed all of it and that no further treatment would be necessary. By Tuesday morning lab tests would settle the issue. When those results came in, however, Jay was in for the biggest jolt of his ordeal. The tests revealed Jay's cancer had spread to his lymph system and totally penetrated the wall of his colon. The oncologist recommended a one-year chemotherapy treatment begin as soon as Jay had recuperated from surgery.

"What are my odds of survival?" Jay asked, shakily.

"You have a forty percent to fifty percent chance of surviving the next two years," the doctor replied.

And so began a phase of life Jay and Diana neither expected nor wanted. "It was a very difficult day for the family, and in particular for my wife, who now had to deal with a very uncertain future," Jay said. "Diana and I had been married for thirty-two years and enjoyed a wonderful marriage. She is one of those rare, godly wives who took great pride in being home with the children and in always keeping the home in incredible order. She was always home for the children when they returned from school and had dedicated her life to being an outstanding wife and mother. To her, the thought of facing life on her own was overwhelming. Her first words to me after learning about my odds of survival were, 'Am I going to have to go get a job?'" Jay assured her that their financial house was in order. She declared through tears that he had always taken such good care of her that she didn't know how she would get along on her own.

*A*fter the shock of the grim diagnosis, Jay and Diana began to reflect on the years preceding their frightening new battle. The Lord's hand, leading, and preparation quickly became obvious.

When Jay and Diana returned to church, they discovered their pastor was nearing the end of a study on the book of Job. By chapter 38 a deeply suffering Job has finished demanding that God answer a long list of questions. God then speaks, but instead of providing Job with any answers, he asks his own questions: "Where were you when I laid the foundation of the earth! Tell Me, if you have understanding, Who set its measurements, since you know? On what were its bases sunk? Or who laid its cornerstone?" Two chapters later a freshly enlightened Job responds, "Behold, I am insignificant; what can I reply to Thee? I lay my hand on my mouth." Jay and Diana instantly saw how the text applied to them. God was saying, "I created this entire universe—don't you think I can handle your simple physical affliction?"

The couple began to recognize God's hand of preparation in other ways, too. Just the year before, they had completed a major financial plan, including a revision of their insurance policies. Because they were contemplating a move to a new home, they had reduced their debt and sold a second home in Flagstaff. They had occupied their new home for just seventy-five days when Jay entered the hospital.

"Had we not sold our Flagstaff home," Jay said, "we likely would have been there at the time and would not have enjoyed the benefit of care from nearby Mayo Clinic."

Just a few days after Jay returned from his ten-day stay at the hospital, his financial planner, Don Christensen, came for a visit. Jay will never forget his words to Diana: "I want you to know that I am praying for Jay's complete recovery; but if he doesn't make it, I know where everything is, and I'll be here for you." Comforting words to a wife terrified at the changes life had brought her way.

Yet another clear example of God's hand in Jay's illness occurred the week he was scheduled to start a further round of chemotherapy. His oncologist called to say he had just returned from a medical seminar that dealt with Jay's type of cancer. Attendees were informed of the results of a long-term study involving the very chemo drugs Jay was taking, and while its results had not yet been published, it concluded that twelve months of chemotherapy were no more effective than six. Jay had just taken the last treatment of his first six months of chemo. Had the doctor not attended that seminar—or had the study, which began in the late 1980s, begun just six months later—Jay probably would have been required to undergo another six months of the dreaded treatment.

On July 11, 1995, I spoke with Jay for the first time and tried to provide some comfort by helping him to understand that others had faced the same situation which now confronted him—and God was faithful in providing the strength to persevere.

Although attending church after his hospital stay physically drained Jay, it also furnished him with new reserves of strength. "I got real emotional when they sang some of the old songs of faith, and I couldn't figure out why I was so deeply moved," he admits. "Then I remembered myself as a young child singing those same songs in church with my family, and I realized that these songs embodied for me the reality of my faith. It was a faith that stretched through generations, from my great-grandparents to my grandparents to my parents. I observed firsthand how this faith makes a difference." All this gave Jay tangible evidence of God's hand in his battle with cancer.

Yet there were also difficulties. One of the frustrating parts of his cancer fight were the questions thrown his way. Christians tended to ask, "Do you ever get mad at God or question why he would allow this to happen to you?" While Jay makes room for honest questions, he says his mind never traveled down that dark path.

Jay points to the "Faith Hall of Fame" in Hebrews 11 and notes that while everyone enshrined in the hall is lauded for genuine faith, their lives took many different turns. Some through faith conquered kingdoms, shut the mouths of lions, quenched the power of fire, escaped the edge of the sword, put foreign armies to flight—while others were tortured, mocked, scourged, imprisoned, stoned, sawn in two, and put to death with the sword. What radically different outcomes of faith! Yet verse 39 says, "And *all* these, having gained approval through their faith, did not receive what was promised, because God had provided something better for us." Jay knows God has something "better" for him laid up in heaven, so his struggles on earth don't seem so overwhelming.

By contrast, the question most frequently asked by unchurched people was, "Can you sleep at night, knowing that you may be facing death?" The thought of death terrorized these folks. Yet Jay found that his cancer provided many opportunities to share his faith in Christ; the real possibility that he might soon die gave his testimony great credibility. One gentleman who never read much of the Bible spoke freely about what he thought it took to get to heaven. Finally, Jay stopped him, looked him in the eye, and asked if he could be completely honest.

"Sure," the man said.

"I've got cancer," Jay replied, "and I've got a forty to fifty percent chance of surviving the next eighteen months. Now, if you were in my shoes, where would you like to place your odds—with what the Word of God says, or what you think it takes to get to heaven?"

The man paused and said quietly, "I see your point!"

In April 1997 Jay wrote to me, "My eighteenth-month checkup showed no sign of cancer. I have now completed one of the alternative therapies. The unfortunate thing is, you never know whether the chemo or alternate therapy has worked; you only know when it hasn't! Beyond that, if the cancer doesn't return, was it the prayer, surgery, chemo, or alternate *therapy? Only the Lord knows, and I have determined that is good enough for me."*

It's now 1998 and Jay's still in remission. Many want to know how Jay can remain so upbeat when facing a possible early death. For these people Jay points to scriptures such as this one: "O our God . . . we are powerless before this great multitude who are coming against us; nor do we know what to do, but our eyes are on Thee" (2 Chronicles 20:12 NASB). The promises of God provide the answers, Jay says, adding, "There is a certain excitement to see what God is going to do, no matter what the outcome. The one charge I would like to leave with my children and grandchildren is the same one given by Moses, Joshua, David, and Solomon: to love the Lord their God, to serve him with a whole heart and a willing mind. Not much else really matters."

8

SONGS IN THE OPERATING ROOM

*T*wo months after he underwent surgery to remove a brain tumor, Jan and I spoke to Brian Wilkes to encourage him in his battle with cancer. It was clear from the start that both Brian and his wife, Natalie, were strong Christians who yet struggled with the uncertainties of such a frightening disease. Nevertheless, Brian had given the whole matter over to God and prayed that his will would be done. He learned through his ordeal that God really is in control, even when it doesn't seem like it. And Brian's story continues to unfold.

On Monday morning, March 10, 1997, building contractor Brian Wilkes arrived at his construction site to frame a two-story building. He expected trusses to show up that day and so was walking atop a second story wall, marking where each should be nailed truss. As a light snow began to fall, he stepped on an unsecured beam which immediately fell out from under him. His right leg hooked on a railing, flipping him upside down and the left side of his head struck the garage wall, twelve feet below. Then his body flipped right side up and dropped another eleven feet, where he crash landed in the dirt, feet first. The impact knocked Brian out for several minutes; the first thing he remembers after regaining consciousness were the wails of an ambulance siren.

A man across the street saw Brian fall and was first on the scene. He later reported Brian didn't breathe for what seemed like a long time. Only after several anxious moments did the contractor suddenly take a big gulp of air, gurgle, and then start to take in air.

At the hospital doctors at first found nothing wrong with Brian except some minor compression fractures in his back. Yet because of his blackout they ordered a CT scan. The test revealed a small tumor growing near the area of Brian's brain that controls his right arm, hand, and leg. Brian was devastated; with four kids ages eight to three and one "surprise" child on the way, what would happen to his family? How could God allow this?

Surgery was scheduled for March 27, but before that Brian asked the elders and several members of his church to lay hands on him and pray that God would do a miracle. During an MRI just hours before his scheduled surgery, Brian fully expected the tumor to have miraculously vanished. But it hadn't; its dark mass still appeared on the view screen. Brian heard the bad news at 8:30 A.M. and had until almost 1:00 P.M. to think about what kind of God he had been serving for seventeen years. The bottom almost fell out of his life. Dark questions filled his mind and a fierce debate raged inside his head.

"I thought, *There must not be a God. Science is right—we're all here just by chance,*" Brian said. "But then I would argue back, *I just can't deny there is a God because of the evidence of the resurrection of Christ. And also the historical fact of over a million Jews walking out of slavery in Egypt without a sword or weapon.* I also thought of all the prophecies Christ had to fulfill. But then I would honestly wonder, *If there is a God in heaven, then why is he forgetting about me?* I kept remembering the whole resurrection story. Finally I concluded, *He is up there—but just who is he?* I told myself I didn't deserve this and if God was my loving heavenly Father, then why had he allowed this to happen to me? I was as scared as I've ever been."

In the heat of his mental battle, Brian was wheeled into surgery.

In days to come Brian would conclude that it was his own prayers uttered weeks before that ignited his intellectual conflict. In his prayer journal the previous February he had written, "Who are you, God? Show yourself to me. Draw me closer and reveal more of yourself to me. Come down and intervene in my life." At the time he thought he was asking for God's help in the sale of a house that had remained on the market for almost a year—he never imagined the answer he would get.

Brian awoke in the operating room as technicians removed equipment. He checked to see if his right hand and foot could move—they did—and he burst into a hymn. "To God be the glory, great things he has done, " he sang as loudly as he could, filling the operating room with the first stanza of that great hymn. "I have never felt the presence and the grace of God in my life as I had at that moment," Brian says. When he finished that song he burst into another, his favorite: "Victory in Jesus, My Savior Forever." The recovery room nurse joined him for both hymns. Then, Brian started preaching to everyone in the room—how he had fallen yet didn't get seriously hurt, how the tumor was discovered. Brian felt "fired up" to be alive and moving, so much so that even his surgeon got a sermon.

After patiently listening to Brian's fervent testimony, the doctor told Brian that most of the tumor that could be seen under the microscope had been removed. In a better-than-expected surgery, ninety percent of the tumor was cut out. Most of its mass could be removed, but not the "fingers" that extended into surrounding tissue. Before the operation this surgeon believed that at least seventy-five percent of the tumor could be removed. With such good news ringing in his ears, aides wheeled Brian up to his room; while still down the hall, he heard the familiar voices of family members. Brian wept with joy.

The pathology report later dimmed some of that joy, but did not destroy it. The pathologist labeled the tumor—a growth about the size of a man's thumb from the knuckle to the tip—an anaplastic astrocytoma, grade three. Yet even that news couldn't steal Brian's hope. He had come through major surgery and major doubts with an increased faith in God, and he wasn't letting go of it.

He no longer asks, "Why are you letting this happen to me, God?" but now declares, "You have been extraordinarily gracious to me, God, to protect me through this process like you did. I don't deserve life at all because I turn my back on you and push you out of the way, yet you still spared my life. I can't understand all your justice and all your grace, but I'm beginning to grasp some little parts of it. It seems as if I have drawn a picture on a chalkboard of who I thought God was and he erased all of it except the justice and the grace part, and he enhanced those two parts. I think I now understand a little of why Moses at the burning bush asked God how he should identify God to Pharaoh. God told Moses to call him 'I AM.' Now I know 'HE IS'! He is present always, and has final control!"

Brian believes God's sovereign control extends to events before his diagnosis as well as after it. A few weeks before he fell off the house, two couples in his church had been asked to start a support group for members struggling with cancer. Brian became the first participant to benefit from the group. Weeks before his accident, the group's leaders had scheduled its first meeting ... for one week after his fall. One leader knew all about brain tumors, having had two of them removed three years earlier. Yet today this woman walks and talks normally after both brain surgery and radiation treatment. It's "coincidences" like this convince Brian that God does perform miracles.

Brian has created a coloring book about his accident for all his kids. He drew an angel holding him with a rope, along with similar scenes, to teach his children about God's grace, about how doctors would not have found the tumor unless he had fallen. This book has helped his children to ask questions about life and death and has enabled them to gain some understanding of the situation.

Many things also have come together in Brian's mind. During his two months of fervent prayer before the fall, he said God showed him his construction work had become too important. The

Lord made it clear to him that his goals were wrong; he wanted to become the best builder in Spokane, but to reach that goal he had to spend more than sixty hours a week on the job. He discovered God was more interested that he become an expert *family* builder.

"I try to make the most of every day now with my wife and kids," he says. "It is much easier to get out of bed with a good attitude, believe it or not. Now I'm very aware of my mortality, as well as the joy of understanding God's grace to me. I don't deserve life, yet he has given it to me!"

Brian attended the huge Promise Keepers' gathering in Washington, D.C., in October 1997, then spent several days for special tests at Duke University, where his best friend from high school is a doctor. Brian had been suffering night seizures that affected the right side of his body and began taking anti-seizure medications. Although the Mayo Clinic rediagnosed the tumor as grade two, Brian's case is still considered terminal. Radiation can control this kind of cancer but rarely eradicates it; and even benign tumors, if they continue to grow, will cause death. Natalie, Brian's wife, is praying that God will bless them with enough years so Brian can help raise all five of his kids. We're joining her in those prayers.

9

SOMETHING TO CAMPAIGN FOR

I met Tim Leslie several years ago at the home of Chuck Collings, president of Raley's Supermarket chain in Sacramento, California. The Collings' clan had gathered a group of friends to hear my testimony and learn about the ministry of the Outreach of Hope. It was a great time— made better by a solid round of golf!

None of us at the time knew about the challenges that lay ahead for Tim—but then, that's life, isn't it?

About thirty years ago Tim Leslie's church asked him to give a ten-minute talk about his relationship with the Lord. Although he didn't want to do it, he finally agreed because he thought it would be good for him. He spoke of how good God had been to him through his growing up years and early married life, when he enjoyed many achievements and much happiness and success. He finished his talk by encouraging his audience to "think about God." His last line still brings an embarrassed blush to his cheeks: "Thinking about God is probably all he really wants of us, anyway."

Today Tim is certain that "thinking about God" is *not* all the Lord wants of us—but he also knows that such thinking may start a chain reaction of events that can change a man's life. And he points to his own life as Exhibit A.

"Thinking about God" first led Tim to join a noontime fellowship group of discussion and prayer; a few years later he and a few other lobbyists organized a prayer breakfast fellowship. As time passed Tim looked for a new job, but not one that would merely satisfy himself. He began seriously praying for what God might want for him. In January 1980 he left his job as a successful legislative representative with a dependable monthly paycheck to become a commissioned real estate salesman. At the same time he decided to run for the Sacramento County Board of Supervisors to fill an unexpected vacancy. Tim won the primary but lost a hotly contested run-off election. But that was the least of his problems.

Suddenly Tim found himself in debt; his run for office had exhausted his family's reserves and he gradually realized how profoundly he had risked his family's future. After eighteen years of stability, Tim and his wife, Clydene, were seemingly alone and in debt with only their own resolve to rely upon. He thought he had been doing the right thing; what had gone wrong? Late one night after Clydene and his two children had gone to bed, Tim sat down all alone in a pitch black living room to pray. With tears streaming down his cheeks he called out to God, "In case there is any question about where I stand with you, I want it clarified. I open my life to you, and want you and me to be in a personal relationship with one another—with you in control. Jesus, I don't know if I am already 'saved' or not, but I don't want any more questions about it from this point forward."

That night Tim gained the assurance that he was not really alone. Despite his fears, God filled him with the beautiful knowledge that he was with Tim. That confidence gave Tim the courage to listen when the Republican Party came calling in 1984. Party officials convinced Tim to run for the State Assembly and he spent a year in the effort— this time losing by nine tenths of one percent. He thought it strange that he would lose when he was so sure God wanted him to run for office, but today he believes he just wasn't yet ready for the job. He had more to learn.

Tim ran again in 1986 and this time it seemed likely he would win. As the election began to wind down, he started complaining about serious pain in his right shoulder; what he thought was pulled ligaments turned out to be a broken clavicle. About a month before election day, his doctor told Tim he needed an operation to remove a cyst in his shoulder. It turned out the "cyst" was a malignant tumor, probably some form of multiple myeloma—and if that was the cause, Tim was informed, he could expect to live only two more years. Multiple myeloma strikes about 13,500 people each year and can be slow, well-behaved, or much more aggressive. "Some more tests will be needed," his doctor said. "Come back next Tuesday and we will tell you what type it is."

With election victory just thirty days away, Tim left the doctor's office that day wondering if he'd be a one-term assemblyman. Yet despite his fear, he knew God was in control. *If I have two years*, he thought, *then God, help me make the most of it. Think what a message I will have for Christ in that two years!*

On Tuesday Tim learned he had beaten the odds and the cancer was localized. After radiation treatment he was given a clean bill of health and was elected to the Assembly. Tim is an ardent conservative who strongly opposes gambling and the California Lottery; he also wants to amend the state Constitution to require minors to get parental permission for abortions. When it came time to be sworn into office, he stood on the sidewalk in front of the state capitol and prayed with a friend. Then he asked, "I wonder what I am supposed to do as I try to take Christ to the capitol?" Tim considers his friend's next words some of the best advice he's ever received. "Tim," his friend replied, "why try to TAKE Christ to the capitol? Why don't you just BE Christ at the capitol?"

Those profound words deeply touched Tim. Yet how could someone do that? After much thought, Tim realized that if Christ lived in him through the Holy Spirit, then he must simply keep Christ at the center of his life and then *go live his life*. Since Christ lived in him, he took the Lord wherever he went—to the halls of the capitol, as he traveled through his district, or even to the privacy of his home.

Tim tried to live out that philosophy in his five years in the Assembly. He joined the Legislature's weekly Bible study group and quickly became known as a round-faced, bespeckled "nice guy" who nevertheless owned a killer political drive. A personal friend and political opponent, Senator John Vasconcellos, said of Tim, "When he first arrived here, he was one of these dogmatic Christian Boy Scout types who had all the truth and thought everybody else was a heretic. But he let go of that. He became open and vulnerable to other people and points of view."[1] In 1991 Tim was elected to the State Senate, representing the northeastern quarter of the state. He's now served the people of California for more than eleven years, and in 1997 he decided it was time for a new challenge and so began an unofficial run for statewide office. He geared up his campaign for Lieutenant Governor . . . and then discovered his cancer had recurred in a more serious form. In April he slipped on some stairs at home and diagnostic X-rays revealed the cancer had reappeared in his shoulder.

The media took note. People run for office all the time, but not people diagnosed with cancer. Remember the attention directed toward the late Paul Tsongas, a former Massachusetts senator, when he ran for president in 1992? Tsongas unsuccessfully tried to defuse worries about his battle with lymphoma by airing TV ads showing him swimming the butterfly. When a reporter for the *Los Angeles Times* asked Tim about his own battle with cancer, the senator replied, "I fully expect to have a future, and I want to spend that future as lieutenant governor. Yes, I have multiple myeloma, and no, it's not fun. But I'm dealing with it and I don't see any reason to quit."[2]

For four days a month while campaigning in the fall of 1997, Tim wore a dispenser on his hip which dripped cancer-fighting drugs into his system. A fellow California legislator, Democratic assemblyman Dick

Floyd, told Tim he'd be willing to admit him to the "bald man's caucus" if his hair should fall out.

"This is my dream," Tim says of his run for lieutenant governor, "And without being overly religious or schmaltzy, I believe I'm doing what God wants me to do."[3]

Doing what God wants him to do is paramount for this state senator. In fact, Tim's life philosophy can be summed up in a neat little sentence: "The whole deal is Jesus Christ."

"It isn't Christ plus America, and it isn't Christ plus community service," he says. "It isn't Christ plus the prayer breakfast, or Christ plus a Bible study. It isn't Christ plus world peace, or Christ plus the fight for the family, or even Christ plus the Republican Party. It is Christ alone. Period."

In an e-mail explaining his cancer fight to loyal supporters, Tim wrote, "God has given me a great vision for Lieutenant Governor—to use this post as a way to reach a new generation of leaders. These are the ones that we older people will turn the reigns of leadership over to. I feel a tremendous burden in my heart to spend time with them—as a friend, an example. To live life with them and to encourage them to great ideas of faith and values. This is for the future of our grandchildren, and for our land."

After four months of mobile chemotherapy, Tim received two more chemo treatments at Stanford University Medical Center. Then in the first week of November, Tim's stem cells were harvested from his blood in a process called aphersis. While the average aphersis takes two to five days, Tim produced enough cells in a single day for a successful bone marrow transplant, which took place the day after Christmas. "I can't think of a better Christmas present than the gift of life," he exclaimed. He then spent two and a half weeks in an apartment across from the hospital, where he was monitored twice a day. In mid-January he returned home, wearing a mask to ward off infections that his weakened immune system could not yet fight. Even then he was eager to get back to the campaign trail; he planned to make his candidacy official in February and had nineteen fund raisers scheduled to begin in March.

But even in the middle of recovering from a bone marrow transplant and running an expensive political campaign, Tim seeks to remember and act on his personal credo: "The whole deal is Jesus Christ." So it should be no surprise that before his transplant, Tim wrote to his friends and supporters, "The thought of suffering through this experience during the blessed Christmas season fills me with anticipation that my walk with the King of kings will grow to an even deeper level."

It's obvious that Tim's battles, whether political or medical, aren't over. (They never are for any of us.) But as long as we remember that "the whole deal is Jesus Christ," we'll all end up winners. And that's something to campaign for.

Tim outpolled two Republican opponents in the June 2, 1998, election for Lieutenant Governor of California. By September 1997, he had raised more than $1 million for his campaign, well ahead of projections. Tim says, "If I just get the cancer vote, I've got this election won!"[4]

Notes

1. Jenifer Warren, "The Races of His Life," *Los Angeles Times*, September 25, 1997, A23.
2. Warren, A3.
3. Ibid.
4. Ibid.

10
A CHRISTMAS TO REMEMBER

When Janet Ferguson's health began to deteriorate, she started asking herself the same accusing question that some ancient religious leaders asked Jesus when they came upon a man born blind: "Who sinned, this man or his parents, that he was born blind?" (John 9:2). The lesson Jesus taught his audience that day bears striking similarities to the insights Janet gained in the past few years. But those insights didn't come easily.

Janet Ferguson has called Jesus her friend ever since she was young. A shy and often quiet girl, she would talk with him and tell him her fears, her problems, and her hopes. Yet she was a worrier and at age nineteen was diagnosed with ulcerative colitis. "If you don't change your ways," doctors warned her, "you'll have to have a colostomy." She did change and began to gain back the weight she had lost.

Janet believed she had left her medical woes behind—and so was surprised in the summer of 1985 when she awoke on a camping trip to excruciating abdominal pain and severe nausea. The attacks occurred periodically for the next six months, then subsided. But at a New Year's celebration in 1987, another attack forced her to leave a party early; three days later she found herself on her kitchen floor in so much pain she didn't know what to do.

A trip to the emergency room led to gall bladder surgery on January 9, but even after recovering from the operation Janet couldn't get her energy back. Her sister, a nurse, noticed Janet's yellowing eyes at Easter services and told her to see a doctor immediately. When a battery of tests could not disclose the cause of her pain, Janet asked God, "Have I been so bad that you are punishing me?" In childhood she had been taught to always do the right thing and be honest, or God would punish her. *Something has caught up with me,* she thought. *Maybe there were times I wasn't honest and didn't do exactly what I should have.* She draws an entirely different conclusion today; now she believes God was simply trying to get her full attention.

Janet traveled to the Cleveland Clinic for an ERCP, a procedure in which doctors snake a tiny camera down the throat to peer inside a patient's bile ducts. On May 5, 1987, Janet learned she suffered from primary sclerosing cholongitis, a rare liver disease which causes inflammation and scarring of the liver bile ducts, narrowing them and damaging the organ. At the time only 100 cases had been reported in ten years. Worst of all, no cure exists for the disease. The doctor told Janet he could do nothing for her.

Janet couldn't believe the news. "I have two daughters, the youngest only five years old," she cried, "and you're telling me I'm not going to be here for them?" She burst into tears, sobbing uncontrollably. On the long drive back home with her husband, Janet kept wondering, *What will I tell my parents and my precious daughters?* She asked God to give her the strength and will to face whatever lay ahead, but decided to say nothing to her children just yet; every time she looked at her two beautiful girls, she broke down into sobs. Why would God want to take her from them?

A special medical consultation a few days later gave her no hope, but she decided to seek the opinion of the family doctor, Dr. Joseph Gregori, a gastroenterologist. "We are not going to sit here and do nothing," he told her. "Let's give a new, experimental procedure a try." This was Janet's first ray of hope. When she arrived home that day, she announced—uncharacteristic for her—"I want no tears, no sympathy, no one feeling sorry for me. I want your prayers and your strength and encouragement to fight this battle. But I repeat: no crying." About the same time her husband, Tom, also adopted a remarkable new outlook. His growing concern worried Janet, but one day while making deliveries he cried out to God, "I don't know what else I can do. Lord, I turn this whole thing over to you. Please help us!" Immediately he felt a deep sense of peace and comfort.

When Tom arrived home he put his arms around his wife and said, "Janet, I know everything is going to work out. It will be OK."

By then Janet was very jaundiced and had lost a great deal of weight. She began taking an experimental combination of powerful medications and Dr. Gregori monitored her blood counts carefully. Gradually the tests showed improvement, Janet's coloring returned to normal, and Dr. Gregori said he thought the disease was starting to arrest itself. Eventually he weaned Janet off all medication.

With her physical improvement, Janet and Tom also sought greater strength for their souls. They began attending Glenwood Primitive Methodist Church, where they found loving people who emphasized prayer and the Word of God. They both began growing spiritually in a way they had never known—a blessed thing, since they would soon face the challenge of their lives.

In late 1993 Janet returned to Dr. Gregori, complaining of fatigue, tenderness in her liver area, and increasing jaundice. He immediately admitted her to the hospital and called in a liver specialist, Dr. Sayad Yossef. Tests seemed to show a tumor in the main bile duct leading to Janet's liver. "I have to be honest," Dr. Yossef admitted to the Fergusons, "it doesn't look good. The probability is great that it's cancerous"—often the end result of this disease.

The night before another ERCP was scheduled to take place, even Tom couldn't comfort his wife. As she brooded alone, she picked up her Bible and randomly opened it to Psalm 121:7— "The LORD will keep you from all harm—he will watch over your life." Instantly she knew she wasn't really alone. "I could feel his presence and his feeling of comfort through the Scriptures," she said. "I felt such a peace. I realized my Lord was in charge and would never leave me. It would all be up to him."

During the procedure the next morning, the hospital's electricity failed twice and the examination took so long that Janet's anesthetic wore off and she began gagging on the tube threaded down her throat. Still, there was good news; no tumor was present, although it was clear the disease was progressing rapidly. Janet would need a liver transplant or she would not survive.

In May 1994 Janet was accepted as a candidate for a new liver. She received a pager to be carried at all times and her condition was monitored closely. The next September the hospital called to say it might have a liver for her, but a fever she was running eliminated her as a candidate. *I wonder if the next call will come in time,* she thought, then checked herself: *This just wasn't the right time; God isn't ready for me. Be patient!*

To prevent a recurrence of this event, doctors put Janet on a maintenance dose of antibiotic to ward off infection and fever. At church she sat in the last row, trying to avoid as many germs as possible, and in October 1995 she attended an "awesome" healing service at her church. "I could feel God touching me as the men of our church laid hands on me and each of them prayed aloud for me," she said. "Then the pastor prayed and anointed my head with oil. My heart was filled with so much love and a sense of hope." The Fergusons began attending a Bible study led by a church friend battling cancer and Janet gained a deeper understanding of how God does things in his timing, not ours.

By Thanksgiving Janet was tired and jaundiced once more. She loved having her family around her and every family gathering became precious. "I tried not to imagine next year and maybe not being here," she said. "When I began to think these thoughts, I would focus on the Lord. Sometimes I even found myself singing 'Turn your eyes upon Jesus, look full in his wonderful face.'"

By Christmas season Janet learned that donor livers were scarce; the previous year, 140 potential recipients had died while waiting for a liver. Still, Janet tried to continue life as normal. She went shopping with a dear friend, wrapped Christmas gifts, hung wreaths, helped decorate her tree, even baked Christmas cookies. On Christmas Eve day she and her sister cleaned shrimp, baked two pecan pies, and made a breakfast casserole for Christmas brunch. That night she attended a Christmas Eve candlelight service—her favorite celebration of all. She and her family returned home about 9:00 P.M., quickly started some Christmas music, then lit the fireplace. At 9:30 the phone rang and a voice on the other end said the Presbyterian Transplant Hospital had a potential liver; he would call back with details at midnight. In minutes the Ferguson home was filled with friends and family who came to pray. Janet's pastor, Bill Vasey, showed up with duffelbag in hand and said, "I'd like to come to Pittsburgh with you, if it's OK." Everyone got in a circle and prayed for God's hand to be on Janet. And at 12:30 A.M.—Christmas morning, 1995— the phone rang and Janet was told to "come now."

On the quiet ride into Pittsburgh Janet noticed a lighted cross atop a snow-covered hill. As she prayed for God's comfort she recalled how the wise men must have felt when they saw a light guiding them to the Christ child two thousand years before. Great reassurance flooded her soul. When she arrived at the hospital, Janet noted a station wagon parked outside with the letters C.O.R.E. painted on its side—an organ procurement agency. Her family and friends got in a circle and prayed again, and by 9:00 A.M. she was wheeled into the operating room and anesthetized. Just before slipping into unconsciousness she prayed that God would guide the hands of her surgeons. "And Lord," she prayed, "wrap your arms around me and hold onto me, ever so tightly." Then she fell asleep.

Her surgery took eleven and a half hours and went extremely well. She spent only forty-eight hours recuperating in the Intensive Care Unit, when many others stay there up to seven days. Her father later told a newspaper reporter, "This is the best Christmas gift I have ever had in my eighty-five years."

As soon as she was able, Janet started walking and quickly wore out a pair of slippers. She made of point of trying to encourage other patients on her floor. One day she walked into a waiting room and saw a young woman sobbing with her mother. Even though the woman had traveled from Boston to see her father in Intensive Care, she couldn't bear to see him as he lay amid a tangle of tubes and machines. Janet told the young woman that just seven days previously she herself had been hooked up just like her dad—and yet now she was walking on her own. The woman's mother later thanked Janet for giving her daughter the strength to visit her father.

Janet's struggles were not over, however. On the sixth day after surgery she began running a fever when her body started to reject its new liver. She was given strong medications that caused horrifying hallucinations, but they did their work. In three more days doctors sent her back to her own room. Her surgeon, Dr. Hiro Furukawa, came to see her every day, "sometimes looking so tired himself, I felt he needed my bed more than I did," Janet said. A nurse's aide also visited every morning, singing praises to God. Janet finally was sent home on January 13, 1996.

"My life was completely changed," Janet says. "I would never or could never be the same. I don't think you can be when you know that you have been touched by the hand of God. And I know I have been."

Since the surgery Janet has done well, with some setbacks. She is now a volunteer educator for Life Banc, an organ procurement agency in northeastern Ohio. She works alongside Tom in their family business and the couple attends a home group study called Friendship with God. In 1996 Tom and Janet not only attended their church's Christmas cantata, they sang in it. "It was glorious, praising God through music," Janet exclaimed. "I sang entirely from my heart. I can't give him enough praise for how he has worked in my life."

PART TWO

THE STRENGTH TO SUFFER

11

YOU DON'T NEED TWO FEET
TO STAND TALL

I doubt I have ever met someone with more enthusiasm and zest for living than Tracy Keeth. And yet I also doubt I've ever met someone who has suffered more pain and handled it so well. In fact, it almost seems her "vocation" is to suffer—and she does it better than anyone we've ever known. When I read the apostle Paul's words, "For it has been granted to you on behalf of Christ not only to believe on him, but also to suffer for him," I can't help but think of Tracy. She does suffer—but she uses that suffering to serve Christ. I think you'll see what I mean.

No matter who you are, you can be certain that you *will* face trials. The only question is, will you *go* or *grow* through those trials? That's the question Tracy Keeth is apt to direct to anyone who inquires about her own excruciating set of circumstances.

Tracy suffers from a rare form of arthritis called Reiter's Syndrome. She has spent thousands of hours in hospitals in Springfield, Missouri, and Kansas City, and also at the Mayo Clinic in Rochester, Minnesota. Because her case is unusually severe, she has become something of an expert on pain.

Her journey of suffering began at age fifteen when her right leg swelled up and became painful to the touch. For two years the pain and swelling grew worse, until at age seventeen her right leg and foot from the knee down had bloated to about three times the size of her other leg. Pain ruled her life. Even a bed sheet brushing against the swollen limb sent waves of pain through her. The pain was so intense she would get headaches from clenching her teeth.

Doctors tried everything to ease her suffering, from inserting a catheter containing pain medication into her spine, to using a cream loaded with cayenne pepper. Nothing worked. Tracy went to physical therapy two hours a day for a year, but still her pain and swelling worsened. She visited some of the most famous hospitals in the country, yet no one seemed to have the answer. One doctor would tell her about a miracle drug or surgery; the next day he'd say, "We're sorry, you are not a candidate for this type of treatment."

At night she heard trains rush by her bedroom window and she would think how easy it would be to end her life and stop the pain. "I thought it would be nice just to die," she says. But just when she thought she could no longer go on, God stepped in.

"Before all this happened I thought I was a Christian, but I wasn't," Tracy admits. "I would attend church when convenient and pray when a problem came up. Now, I know God and he walks with me. God through his grace keeps me going."

When the pain became unbearable, Tracy would think of the pain Jesus suffered when he was beaten, spit upon, and crucified. Many sleepless nights she spent praying and studying the Bible. And that brought her closer to God.

Finally her doctor said the veins in her leg had collapsed, cutting off all circulation. Amputation was now the only option. At first she was angry, but after months of suffering she was ready to try anything.

Tracy had several weeks at home to prepare for surgery. "The first week I was in turmoil. I knew the amputation was necessary, yet I thought, *Tracy, if you only had more faith, God would heal your leg*. After praying that I would make the right decision and have the grace to accept it, a calm came over me. I felt peace about the decision to amputate." So on March 5, 1992, she underwent an above-the-knee amputation.

Several weeks later she went to school for the first time that year; her friends at Marshfield High School had been enjoying their senior year while she was homebound with a tutor—an especially sore trial for a highly social athlete like Tracy. Within weeks she started wearing a prosthesis, using crutches for stability. "One of the happiest moments in my life was walking down the aisle at graduation without crutches," Tracy says. "That night I even played basketball and volleyball."

Yet a few months later her other leg began to swell. After exploratory surgery on June 25, 1993, doctors announced that another amputation was necessary. Tracy felt helpless lying in the recovery room after surgery, but sometime late that night a deep peace overwhelmed her as God assured her he was no longer just holding her hand; he was now carrying her. She was convinced everything was going to be fine.

"People may look at me with shock or pity, but I am much happier now—even without legs—because I have a relationship with Jesus," she explains.

The disease is still in her body, however, and continues to cause severe headaches, seizures, and stomach complications. Tracy must be very careful about her diet—she avoids dairy products and fried and spicy foods—but she can't keep much down, anyway. Some days she can't even tolerate water. As a consequence, by 1994 she weighed just seventy pounds. "My stomach's never going to be normal," Tracy admits. "I always have pain. I always have a real bad headache. I'm weak all the time. It seems like I get built back up and then, whammo, it starts again."

Ruth McPhail, a home health nurse who has stayed with Tracy for twelve hours a day, explains that "it's like having arthritis in the blood vessels of your brain. That's why she's in constant pain." To help control the pain Tracy had a nerve stimulator implanted in her abdominal cavity. Beyond that, she must make trips to the hospital every six to eight weeks to receive fluids that replenish her dehydrated body. And how does she respond to all this?

"You could lie around and wallow in self-pity or you can get up and realize that you don't need to have two feet to stand tall,"

Tracy says. "It's going to take a lot to knock me down. Each trial has brought me closer to God."

Still, it's a difficult life. Tracy used to be a fast pitch softball player and loved volleyball, but that's all gone now. "The part I hate the most is missing the sports," she said. "It took me a long time to get over that. It would mean so much to me to be back in sports again. I'm trying to get into wheelchair basketball."

When she feels strong enough, Tracy now spends her free time painting on ceramic, wood, and canvas, mostly in acrylics. She also likes to cook and read. She hopes to write a book about her life and a few years ago she helped to oversee the construction of a handicap-accessible room at the Keeth residence, a project made possible by concerned Marshfield residents. When she turned twenty on June 1, 1994, Tracy received over four hundred birthday cards from people who had learned of her plight. That day the Marshfield Evangelical Methodist Church also presented her with a large birthday banner signed by members of the congregation; balloons and flowers filled her home.

Tracy's mother, Glenda, says, "I just hope and pray that she can go into some kind of remission and be healthy for a long time." But there's little hope of that; no cure exists for the disease and it continues to complicate Tracy's life. A quick review of major incidents since she graduated from high school amply demonstrates that point.

Tracy first enrolled at Southwest Baptist University in Bolivar, Missouri, to pursue her dream of independence by living in a dorm and studying to become a physical therapist, but her illness forced her to leave during her first semester. She is no longer pursuing a career in physical therapy, but someday would like to become a clinical psychologist and a motivational speaker who encourages audiences to set goals and follow God. If anyone has the credibility for such a role, it's Tracy. She speaks like that all the time, whether she has an audience or not.

In January 1995 she caught mononucleosis and by the end of the month had to return to the hospital because of another seizure; intense back pain also suggested she had suffered a compression fracture in her spinal cord. Due to her disease and also because of a lack of exercise, Tracy's bones are soft and her seizures usually break a few bones.

In October 1995 her heart suddenly stopped during a hospital stay. A nurse who happened to walk by noticed she wasn't breathing and began CPR; later she was diagnosed with an electrical heart malfunction and was placed on medication. For eight weeks prior to this incident she had been suffering grand mal seizures[1] which resulted in eight fractured vertebrae. Although Tracy's car is equipped with hand controls for driving, her frequent seizures now prevent her from driving.

In November she moved from the hospital to a care facility, but because her bed rail was not in place, she fell out of bed, broke her hip ("It hurt worse than either of my amputations," Tracy said), and had another seizure. Surgery on her hip was scheduled for Thanksgiving and her family spent the day at the hospital. That month she also began to report dizzy spells that lasted about fifteen minutes.

In January 1996 the fainting spells and seizures were diagnosed as autonomic neuropathy, perhaps triggered by a head injury suffered when she played baseball years before.

In May it was back to the hospital to fight pancreatitis, hepatitis, and a dangerous septis infection in her blood stream.

In August, while back in the hospital, doctors told Tracy's parents that she was going to die. But a "miraculous thing" happened in the intensive care unit after a friend came and prayed for her. Tracy's temperature dropped from 107 to 99, her pain almost disappeared, and she began to feel much better.

In April 1997 Tracy was down to fifty-nine pounds and had to helicopter out of church after a morning service when she suffered yet another seizure; this time she broke some ribs.

Yes, Tracy is something of an expert in pain. Yet she's also a committed witness to Jesus Christ. During her April hospital stay she met John, a man who while driving drunk had killed another driver. She shared the Lord with him and planned to take him to church. She called this hospital visit her "Romans 8:28" ("And we know that in all things God works for the good of those who love him, who have been called according to his purpose"). This incident and others like it have caused her to see each hospitalization as a divine assignment to minister God's love to someone in great need.

When she's able, Tracy speaks to youth groups, women's groups, and many other organizations about what God means to her. "I may not have legs, but that does not stop me from telling of all the wonderful works of God in my life," she says. "Be happy with what life gives you. Never become satisfied with your relationship with the Lord—always strive to grow closer."

Of course, Tracy won't say that she never has moments when she thinks, *Why me?* Sometimes she wishes things could return to how they once were. "But when I do have these feelings, I just turn to the Lord in prayer and he helps me through them," she explains. "I really haven't been that mad. I think God just takes care of that. The courage and the strength, it all comes from God. Each new problem that comes up, you get stronger and stronger instead of every setback making you weaker."

After all, she says, problems on earth are temporary, while eternity is forever. "I have lived life when I really didn't know God," she declares, "and I've lived life when I can't get enough of him. I've seen both sides of the fence. Now that I know him, I can't help but smile when I think about what he has done in my life."

And we can't help but smile when we see what Tracy is doing with her life. Despite her medical trials and frequent hospitalizations, Tracy has recently decided she wants to return to the world of athletics— this time as a high school volleyball coach. Go Tracy!

Notes

1. In a grand mal seizure (French: "great sickness"), the victim loses consciousness and falls to the ground. After the fall the body stiffens, respiration often stops for about a minute, and the victim turns blue; following this, all four extremities jerk spastically. Immediately after the attack the victim is usually confused and sleepy and may have a headache.

12

THE MASK COMES OFF

I first met Dwayne Potteiger at a Unified Christian School fund raising banquet, got better acquainted after one speaking engagement, and really got to know him on a plane flight while en route to another speaking engagement. I learned he was born in Pennsylvania, moved to Africa for a few years with his missionary parents, then later returned to Pennsylvania. Shortly before we spoke, Dwayne had accepted a new position with Kingdom Building Ministries[1] in Denver and had moved his wife and two daughters from San Diego to Colorado.

But that isn't what so captivated me about this man. He was battling brain cancer, yet his deepest desire was to help others reach maturity in Christ. He's known the heat of a gut-wrenching trial by fire, but he keeps trying to put one foot ahead of another and is determined to continue walking in the direction God has called him. But he can tell you the story himself.

"Somebody get a nurse, I need help!" Those were the last words I remember before falling into a grand mal seizure. As I stood before an audience of more than two hundred and fifty people, the room began spinning and I lost consciousness. In a few seconds of semi-consciousness I realized I was in an ambulance, siren blowing, with needles and tubes sticking out of my body. I faded out of consciousness again and when I reawoke I saw my wife leaning over the gurney as I was being rolled from one room to another. "They've found a mass in your brain," she said, then I blacked out once more.

When I regained consciousness, doctors told me surgery would be very dangerous, so they were going to refer to another hospital to see some specialists. Further x-rays and MRIs suggested I might have a brain tumor and I was quickly scheduled for surgery.

A few days later I went under the knife. After a seven-and-a half-hour surgery I was beginning to awaken from a deep sleep when through my mental fog I heard a nurse ask me, "Are you awake? Do you know where you are? What is your name? What day is it? Who is your wife? Can you feel this?" Her questions seemed endless and she demanded answers to each one. "I need you to talk to me!" she commanded.

Over the next several hours I gradually returned to my senses and found my head wrapped in a large, turban-like bandage. Doctors had removed a large egg-sized mass from the rear of my right temporal lobe. The right side of my face was swollen and pain prevented me from opening my mouth. I later learned that the muscles of the jaw and neck on my right side had been removed and then reattached during surgery. Later when I noticed nurses talking loudly and repeating their requests to an unresponsive man in the bed next to mine, I asked, "What kind of surgery did he have?"

"Brain surgery, just like you," a nurse replied. Immediately I thanked God that he had spared me and directed my surgeon's hands.

The day after surgery, a Tuesday, I was moved from the intensive care unit into a regular room. On Wednesday the surgeon took off my bandages and in a mirror I saw a bald, bloodied head with thirty-seven shiny staples holding together an incision that began at my right temple and went up around my head in a half circle and ended at the back of my head. The right side of my face and head were swollen. It was freaky to look at myself.

On Thursday two surgeons entered my room and announced, "We're sorry to tell you that the mass was malignant." They called it a grade 3 anaplastic astrocytoma and gave me fifty weeks to live. I couldn't breathe; it felt like elephants were thundering across my chest. I couldn't think. I felt numb. It seemed as if my words and prayers dribbled out of my mouth and tumbled onto the floor. I felt overwhelmed.

After four days in the hospital I left for my parents' home, where my family stayed for one week as I recovered from surgery. When we returned home to San Diego we arranged to see an oncologist who recommended I begin therapy with a stereotactic radiation procedure (a thread-beamed, intense form of radiation therapy) followed by conventional radiation and one year of chemotherapy.

So at 6:00 A.M. on the day of the stereotactic procedure I arrived at the hospital. Doctors soon began attaching a metal "halo" to my head with four screws, after which I was to be bolted to a table for the radiation treatment. I have never endured such pain! The four Novocain injections I received seemed to do little to blunt the screaming agony of the screws being driven, one by one, into my skull. But the worst was to come. A doctor walked into the room, saw me, and exclaimed, "Oh no! I thought we talked about this before!" The resident internist had attached my halo too low and it would have to be removed and reattached. This time the doctor attached the halo while the interns stood back and watched.

As he began to turn the screws into the back of my head, I lost control of my body. The excruciating pain caused me to flop like a fish out of water; it felt like torture. Each of the four screws was tightened until I thought my head was going to explode.

After waiting for a couple of hours, I was taken to a room where I was bolted to the table, my head and neck suspended by the four screws. The radiation treatment took one and a half hours and the pain grew to the point where I thought I would lose my mind.

Before beginning the six and a half weeks of conventional radiation, I asked for and received a few weeks to recover. When treatment began, for five days a week both sides of my head were shot with radiation. After about two weeks my hair began falling out at the radiation sites and I was left with a weird-looking mohawk. Early in the treatment I also made an unpleasant discovery. I was breathing in as the radiation machine began and immediately smelled burning flesh; after that I held my breath as soon as I heard the machine go on.

Chemotherapy began about two weeks after I finished radiation. Even though I took anti-nausea medication, three to four hours after taking the pills I would get violently sick, getting cold and sweaty at the same time. I gagged and gasped for breath, vomiting so hard that I thought my stomach and intestines would be the next things in the basin. Yet somehow I made it through.

Doctors gave me, at best, a twenty percent chance of surviving three to four years, and at thirty-one years of age, I didn't think that was good enough. I found a book by Anne Frahme titled *A Cancer Battle Plan*, followed her directions, and began juicing and eliminating many foods we had been used to eating. (Doctors had given her up to die but she pursued a natural therapy and within weeks had no sign of cancer. Sadly, I just learned that in the past few weeks the cancer suddenly reappeared and Anne passed away after surviving eight years.) We also pursued treatments in Mexico that are not allowed in the United States; these seemed to help.

Changing our diet as a family took real discipline. We turned from refined and processed products to fresh foods. One evening as we sat down to a dinner of three plates of vegetables, I asked my oldest daughter to pray. "Dear God," she implored, "please help us not to choke. Amen!" The change was hard at first, but gradually we lost our desire for the old staples. The natural foods began to provide a fuller taste—and if I would cheat and snack on a little of the foods we once bought regularly, they would inevitably make me feel sick.

In 1994 we moved to Denver, Colorado, leaving behind everything—doctors, friends, a job with secure salary, and our insurance. It was the hardest thing I have ever done, but God clearly was leading us to move.

After one of my regular check-ups (scheduled for every two to three months) the neurosurgeon decided that five suspicious-looking areas surrounding the previous tumor site had to be removed and so set my second craniotomy for June 1995. Most of the tissue extracted—five nickel-sized masses—turned out to be dead brain cells killed by the radiation treatments; only scattered cancer cells were found.

A few months after my second surgery I began to suffer excruciating headaches; my head felt as if a tribe of drummers were inside trying to get out. An MRI revealed a large mass in the previous resection site; swelling had caused the right side of my brain to push against the left side. Steroids were prescribed to control the swelling, and I began gaining weight. In a third surgery, a mass the size of a large lemon was removed, and again it was identified as necrotic tissue with some scattered cancer cells. I was still dealing with the impact of the radiation treatments I had received almost three years earlier!

And "impact" is exactly the right word. The surgeries and therapies have affected Dwayne in several ways:

Short-term memory. I can't remember things. People laugh and say, "Now you know what it's like when you get old," but it's not funny. It's more difficult now to remember people, places, or things. I have conversations with friends and even go to their homes for dinner and yet remember nothing about the encounters. I feel stupid, even retarded.

Eyesight. I have lost some vision in the left fields of both eyes. When driving I find it difficult to read the street signs until I slow down. The family encourages me to be more careful when I'm behind the wheel. Thankfully, that seems to be getting better over time.

Mental fog. Since this all began I have felt as if I've been in a mist. Life seems unreal. I often feel in a daze, struggling to stay connected with what's real. Time has become a blur because I can't remember sequences. I struggle with a constant feeling of uncertainty.

Depression. I'm not the same person I used to be. To some extent I feel stripped of my identity, forever altered, and unable to change what has happened to me. Some days I just want this whole tiresome journey to end. On the outside I look like the same ol' me, the person I used to be, but inside I feel like someone quite different. Some things now overwhelm me more easily, and I struggle to maintain a normal life. It's as if I have to learn all over again how to manage daily life.

And yet . . . .

Although there are many aspects of this journey that continue to confuse and frustrate me, I have found a new depth in my spiritual life that I would not trade for the world.

First, my condition has prompted me to refocus my energies on life's real priorities.

Our marriage has weathered an incredible storm. Rhonda, my wife, has been an awesome source of strength and stability during this journey and has been an anchor in the midst of the storm. From my three surgeries to carting me to all the treatments and doctor's appointments, she has continually stayed by my side, repeatedly sacrificing her plans and desires to take care of my every need.

Rhonda quit her job to spend untold hours reading and studying in an attempt to learn and do everything she can to provide the best food, the best care, and the best love and encouragement possible. Rhonda has picked up all the pieces of our lives and carried an incredible load—physically, emotionally, and spiritually—through this journey. I marvel at how she can keep so many plates spinning with little to no thought of herself. While doing all this for me, she has tried to maintain a normal life and schedule for our two daughters, Rachel and Erika. She has shown me what real love is. Rhonda Potteiger is a modern-day heroine, and I am honored to have her as my wife.

I have become much more sensitive to my family's needs, both as a unit and as individuals. I'm striving to make some memories for my wife and children that will remain after I'm gone—playing games with the girls, tucking them into bed, talking with them about their day and how school went. I have started writing a journal for each child as a treasured gift.

Second, I have made it a priority to invest in relationships, even if they're long distance. This has become vital to me, an intimate part of my cancer journey. As the value of my friendships has escalated for me, I have tried to remain in contact through e-mail, phone calls, letters, and visits.

Third, this difficult journey has taken away the masks I used to wear to protect me from people seeing my failures and weaknesses. I have become very transparent, even with people I've just met. I try to be open about my journey and my experiences, both good and bad.

Fourth, my compassion for other sufferers and my awareness of the needy around me has greatly increased. I am much more sensitive than I was and I find that tears come quickly to me now. I know more fully what it means to "weep with those who weep."

Fifth, the emptiness of sin and this world's philosophies are clearer to me than ever before and I want nothing to do with them. When the oncologist told me I could expect to live three to four years with treatment, my desire for material things greatly diminished; the sparkle and glitter doesn't dazzle me anymore. I am much more content than I was formerly. Before the cancer, I nurtured goals of climbing the success ladder, of buying a bigger house or fancier car. Now I'm content with simplicity. Material things have paled in importance as my spiritual life has catapulted forward.

And one last thing: although I don't know how long I have to live, the time I do have I live with a much clearer sense of purpose. God's call to personal obedience and holiness has escalated and I am finding that only God can fulfill my deepest longings and needs. I'm more reflective now and know I enjoy a greater intimacy and closeness to God in the midst of my struggle than I ever did before the cancer struck.

Only one thing really matters, and that is knowing Christ as my personal Savior and walking with him in a personal, intimate relationship. In comparison with eternity, all of our lives are very short. I want to do and give my best to building the kingdom of God while I still have the chance.

While Dwayne says he never would have chosen the path he now walks, he wouldn't trade it for the world. He has learned to cultivate "an attitude of gratitude" and spends a lot more time these days marveling at the beauty of God's creation. Birds and flowers, trees and grass, mountains and oceans all fill him with a sense of wonder and thankfulness. He continues to enjoy the many splendors of God's creation as he travels across the country and the globe, speaking to people about their brief time on earth and asking them how they're spending it.

Notes

1. Dwayne works full-time with Kingdom Building Ministries as an itinerant speaker. He is available to speak to churches or organizations by contacting: Kingdom Building Ministries, 14140 E. Evans Ave., Aurora, CO 80014. 1-800-873-8957. Website: www.kbm.org; email: ininerant@kbm.org.

13

THE HAPPIEST TIME OF ALL

Some people respond to life's hardships with such determined optimism that you can't keep yourself from wondering, Is this person for real? *I admit I entertained that thought about Lew Gilbert when I first started hearing from my staff about his incredible response to a difficult medical situation. Now I know he's the real deal. See if you don't come to the same conclusion.*

Lew Gilbert describes life in November 1995 as "abundant and fulfilling." He and his wife, Darlene, were spending a lot of time with their eight grandchildren, traveling, and moving into a new home. Lew was enjoying continued success in his insurance business, serving at church, and responding to everyday situations.

All was going well—except, perhaps, some troubling medical issues. "At sixty-one, a man has to pay a little closer attention to bone aches and general slowing down of physical activity," Lew says. He particularly began to watch a lump that appeared on his sternum.

But perhaps that's not the best place to start Lew's story. Six months prior to this, at a meeting of small group leaders from his church, Lew asked his prayer partner to earnestly pray that he would gain a stronger focus in his personal devotion to God, especially in his personal study and prayer time. Lew felt a deficiency in those areas and felt as though his own prayers didn't seem effective enough to produce the degree and intensity of devotion he wanted to give the Lord.

So the man prayed ... and six months later Lew Gilbert answered his phone and heard his doctor say, "Lew, you have a malignant cancer called multiple myeloma."

Lew does not believe, nor would he ever imply or say, that God *caused* his cancer. "Our God is not that kind of god!" he insists. "I will, however, say that he knew I was going to get cancer. So what did he do? He prepared my heart in such a way that I would be able to deal with it. Praise God!"

On a Wednesday afternoon Lew first learned cancer was going to shadow him the rest of his natural life. Almost from that moment, God provided what Lew calls "a re-run of my life." His mind reflected over many of the major joys and delightful experiences he had been privileged to savor. He thought of Darlene, his dear wife of incredible, selfless character. He pondered three beautiful, Christ-centered children who are rearing their own children with a rich and deep fervor for Christ. He remembered multiple opportunities to serve his Lord and his kingdom. He gave thanks for a successful business, many life-long friends, a balanced life with many interests, and abundant provision for material needs. But most of all, he reveled in a God who showed him what his grace and love are all about. "To this very day," Lew says, "I continue to be fortified by reliving all the wonderful blessings God has provided for us."

Lew sees even chemotherapy treatments as an opportunity to receive—and give—blessings from God. For more than eighteen months he took chemotherapy, along with multiple radiation treatments, to eradicate the lesions and tumors that occur with multiple myeloma. He had heard all the horror stories about the human body's reaction to this form of therapy, but "somehow God has blessed me with none of the physical problems connected with treatments of that nature," he says.

In fact, Lew believes that the most exciting and uplifting experiences he has enjoyed have occurred when he entered the hospital for chemo. His protocol required him to receive six ninety-six hour infusions of continuous drip, cancer-killing chemical agents, and from the time he was admitted to the time he was discharged, he could plan on a stay of nearly five days. Yet he calls these visits "just awesome."

He remembers leaving the hospital the first time he received a ninety-six hour treatment and saying, "You know, I came into this hospital five days ago thinking I was going to receive a chemo treatment. Well, that did happen and now I am leaving the hospital with something far more valuable than what I came in to receive. I am leaving with such a feeling of gratitude to God for putting me in this place where he can be glorified through prayer, praise, music, singing, and hugs. I am grateful that he gives me so many opportunities to receive and share his love through those who serve professionally, those who come to visit, and those who are willing to cross the line to do everything to help lift my burden."

When you hear something like that, and if you're honest, you have to wonder, *This has to be some kind of show, some kind of super spiritual nonsense he's concocted to shield himself from reality. The man has to be in denial. He has to be lying to himself. At the core of his being, he can't really feel this way. Can he?*

Well, I've met Lew and spoken with him many times, and I for one am convinced this is no act. A few members of our staff know Lew better than I do, and they're even more certain that he's absolutely the genuine article. He's not in denial; he's not lying to himself; he's not putting on a show. Our staff uses terms like "walking miracle" and "unbelievable" (in a good sense) and "blessing" to describe Lew. And I think they're right.

Lew truly believes that the hospital has become the place where God gave Darlene and him the opportunity to receive and share his love and grace with others. One evening during his first week in the hospital, Lew's "small group" from church came to visit. A volunteer chaplain happened to be passing by and spent an hour with the group. As the man was leaving he said, "I came into this room to minister and am leaving having been ministered to." To this day, the chaplain remains a great Christian friend of Lew's.

Lew and Darlene have been able to live out their faith by listening to other cancer patients. Other times they verbally share their faith in God through prayer and fellowship. "What a powerful and meaningful experience we have during our hospital visits!" Lew says.

Throughout all Lew's experiences with cancer, his constant prayer is that God will be seen and glorified in everything that happens in his life and in that of his family. The lyrics to a song written by David Michael Carillo express clearly how Lew wants to deal with his disease:

Set my heart aflame Lord
Let it burn in me.
It's a vessel for your honor
I desire to be.
Pour your wine of gladness
Let it flow through me,
That all who taste your goodness
May be drawn to Thee.[1]

After a year of treatments Lew's medical team was able to get his cancer into remission. The next step was to be two bone marrow transplants, but in the time it took him to secure all the necessary medical data and receive approval from his insurance company to go forward with the procedure, his cancer actively returned. In early 1997 he was in the middle of two additional ninety-six hour chemo drips, hoping that his cancer will once more go into remission and thus allow the bone marrow transplant to take place.

Most patients and even doctors would consider what happened to Lew a "setback." And yet Lew (naturally) has a different take on the situation.

"This is how the Lord has encouraged me to think about it," he says. "In our hometown of Indianapolis, an automobile race called the Indy 500 is held each year. It's perhaps the greatest auto race in the world. Darlene and I have enjoyed that exciting event many times over the years, and I got to thinking: many drivers who have won that race did not start in the first row. You can start in the third or even the fourth row and still win the race, as long as you know where you are going, how you are going to get there, have a good crew, a good race car, owner, sponsor and chief mechanic. In our Lord Jesus Christ, I have all of that. The winning of my race is in God's hands and my trust is in him. He will not fail."

And if that analogy doesn't work for you, Lew has another. In 1997 the men's basketball team from the University of Arizona won the NCAA tournament right in Lew's hometown. They came into the Final Four as a number four seed from their region, while the other three teams which made it to Indianapolis all boasted number one seeds. Yet the Arizona Wildcats proved to the basketball world that a team doesn't have to have a number one seed to win it all. Lew expects to win—one way or another. He's especially confident because of his own teammates.

"The prayer support that we have been receiving has been overwhelming," he explains. "We are being blessed through prayers from so many sources—from family, a multitude of wonderful friends, our church, a fourth grader from one of our local Christian schools whom I do not even know, Bible Study Fellowship, prayer chains in many other church bodies from Oregon to New York—even the United Kingdom!—a waitress and her two children, people from the insurance agency I work for, and so many others that my memory can't sometimes recall. The beautiful thing about prayer support is to feel it, to know that it will and does work to the glory of God. God has blessed us with that awareness."

While the disease and treatment of multiple myeloma often overwhelms many patients, Lew seems far more overwhelmed with the support he has received in his battle. "I consider my life and the issues I am dealing with as a true calling from God," Lew says. "God is exercising his will in my life as we press on together.

Time and again, that has been fortified through the multitude of experiences Darlene and I have had since our journey began."

Early in his treatment Lew asked his wife if it were possible for someone to have malignant cancer and yet feel the happiest he had ever been in his life. "Yes," Darlene said, "that is possible."

She knew it was possible, because that was exactly how Lew felt. "Sure, there are times when I wish I didn't have cancer," Lew says, "but all I need to do is to focus on our God and realize that my eternal life began when God chose me and I understood and accepted that miracle. What a God he is!"

Indeed, Lew, what a God he truly is. He'd have to be to create a man like you.

Notes

1. "A Servant's Prayer" by David Michael Carrillo © 1994. The Songs of Gentle Wind (ASCAP) Admin. by Gentle Wind Music Ministry.

14

FINDING TRUE WORTH

The list of medical challenges that have confronted Larry Talley over his lifetime reads like a compilation of incidents from an office full of patients: polio, recurrent cancer, pneumonia, diabetes, heart attacks. Add to that various personal hardships that have been thrown Larry's way, and you have the makings of a tragic story. Yet Larry's story doesn't end in tragedy, even though it is filled with pain.

Larry Talley figures he must have been a good talker even when he was a nine-year-old grade schooler. In a section of an old yearbook from those days he remembers classmates predicted he would become a Baptist minister. That never happened, but to this day some people say he should have been a preacher. With all that he's endured, he'd certainly have the credibility and compassion the job calls for. People tend to believe him when he says something like, "God allows us choices and we can choose to focus on what we have lost or we can focus on what we still have to give. Our worth is not just a sum of what we did in the past, but what we can be for the rest of our lives, no matter how long or short that may be."

There's a ton of freight pulling behind those words. But to appreciate it all you have to go back to March 28, 1944, when a farm couple in rural Missouri welcomed their fifth son into the world. The little boy, Larry Talley, was diagnosed with polio at age two. He spent nine months in the hospital and didn't recognize his mother when she came to take him home. The nurse who cared for Larry all that time asked if she could adopt him, since she had no children of her own and his mother had four other sons. Larry's mother replied by snatching her son and taking him home.

After the disease ran its course Larry was fitted with a full-length brace on his right leg. Since he never knew any other condition, he learned early to adjust. He still wears a brace on that leg.

At the age of seven his family moved to Millersville, Missouri (population fifty-two), and Larry started to play basketball. He couldn't run the court like other boys, but he did develop one of the best long shots on the team. He also worked on a deadly, underhanded free throw style. He and his friends played mostly on dirt courts at first, but in 1957 classes moved into a new school with a real gym. Now Larry had a problem. He wasn't allowed to play on the new, wooden floor because his shoes would leave permanent marks on the court. But he had a solution: he took an old tennis shoe from one of his older brothers and forced it to fit over his brace shoe. Violà! No marks on the court.

In Millersville he also saw his relationships grow strong with both his mother and his God. His mother loved to be his biggest cheerleader. Many times when Larry grew discouraged she told him, "Larry, you can do anything anyone else can do, if you just set your mind to it and ask God for his help when times get really tough. And thank God in all the good times. You'll see, even when tough times come along, God will see you through. Even when Mom and Dad are not around, God will always be by your side. I know God has special things planned for you someday."

In the summer of 1952, God also was watching out for Larry. While Larry's father mowed hay in the bottom fields, Larry rode the side plate on the tractor, something he often did just to be with his dad. One day as evening approached the blades on the mower grew dull, but since only a small patch of one field remained uncut, the pair kept going. Yet it was slow work. The mower frequently clogged up and Larry's dad had to stop the tractor and back it up a few feet while Larry jumped off, dislodged the offending clump of hay, and threw it behind the tractor. Then he'd jump back on and his dad would proceed until the mower clogged up again. This happened several times until Larry's father began to lose patience.

To hurry the process along Larry tried to time his jump from the tractor. But as his dad grew more irritated, Larry changed the stopping pattern and Larry jumped off before he should have. His dad jammed the tractor in reverse so fast that Larry's brace foot got caught beneath the tractor's big rear tire, which rolled over his entire brace leg, smashing it to the ground. Larry screamed, his dad immediately saw what happened and pulled the machine, off his son's leg. He then shut down the tractor, jumped to the ground, pulled Larry's brace leg out of the dirt, and carried his son to a shade tree. As he pulled the brace away from the leg they both saw it was very bruised but not broken. Larry smiled, looked up at his dad and said, "It sure is a good thing that God gave me this brace to wear or I would have had a crushed leg." With tears running down his cheek his father looked back at Larry and replied, "I sure guess that's true, Sonny. Let's go home. This mowing just isn't that important anymore today."

That year Larry raised money for the March of Dimes to pay back what the organization had done to help his parents buy his braces. For several weeks he went into Millersville and collected mostly dimes and nickels in an era when no one had much to spare. Eventually he collected $137—a princely sum for those days—and the local paper printed a photo taken with the doctor who ran the March of Dimes.

And how did Larry get around? He learned to ride a bicycle, pedaling with his left foot only. "I sure had a badly beat up bicycle by the time I got proficient at riding it," he remembers. "But now I had new transportation. I could travel all over, and I did. My mother sometimes was not thrilled when I would forget to tell her my whereabouts. My bicycle was my freedom to see and do all the things young boys do."

When Larry was twelve and in the eighth grade, he began to notice girls. To compensate for his disability—he limped noticeably—he determined to accomplish feats that showed he was a man. He learned to climb a two-story high rope in the school gym without using his legs; only he and two other boys could climb to the ceiling and back using hands only, and Larry climbed the fastest. He also started to lift weights and worked out on a punching bag to improve his coordination. "Again, I was trying to get noticed," Larry says.

As a tenth grader he became the manager of the high school basketball team and put a lot of hours into being the best manager he could be. That's how he earned his first and only "J Club" letter from Jackson High School in Jackson, Missouri. He was to receive his letter at a school assembly along with the other members of the team.

"I was the last to be called for my long work as manager," Larry recalls, "but this day it was not to be; there were no more letters and my name was not even mentioned. All the players looked at me with disappointment in their eyes. Some could not understand what had happened."

Neither could Larry. He went straight home and directly to his room, closed the door, and began to cry. When his father got home, Larry was summoned outside to explain what had so upset him; when he told the tale, his dad lost his temper, grabbed Larry, and marched down to the school, where he confronted a very embarrassed basketball coach. The coach had simply made a mistake and offered Larry his letter on the spot, but the young man didn't want it; what he really wanted was the recognition he had been denied.

A few days later at the conclusion of another school assembly, the principal instructed students and staff to remain seated for one last presentation. A chastened coach walked to the front, apologized for forgetting Larry at the awards assembly, called him "the best manager this team has ever had" and presented Larry with his letter. The whole school cheered.

The following two years Larry didn't manage the basketball team, but he did continue to lift weights and build up his body (to a forty-four inch chest and twenty-nine inch waist) to impress the girls, but he still had trouble getting a date.

In 1962 Larry graduated from high school and followed Paula, the girl of his dreams, to Memphis. He stayed in Memphis for a year and half but when she still was not ready to marry, he left town, leaving behind the love of his life. He didn't think he could continue on as "just friends."

Two years later he returned to Jackson and married a local girl, with whom he had one son and two daughters. He worked with his father in a family business until 1978, when he was divorced and moved to St. Louis. There he bought another business but filed for bankruptcy in 1982, losing everything. For the next four years he worked at any job he could find and felt like a failure. He grew totally discouraged and wondered where God could be.

In 1987, out of the blue, Larry received a phone call from his long-lost love, Paula. From March to October the two phoned and corresponded with each other. Larry was traveling near Memphis as Halloween approached and the two arranged to have dinner to catch up on the past twenty-five years. After the date Larry realized he felt the same love for Paula he had known a quarter of a century before. He returned to his hotel, fell to his knees, and asked God to forgive him from wandering so far from home. He then thanked his heavenly Father for all he had done for him. For the first time in years he sobbed and his heart began to soften. It had been a long time since October 25, 1953, when Larry first accepted Christ at the age of nine and was baptized at the Millersville Baptist Church.

Later that November Larry returned to Memphis, married Paula, and the newlyweds moved to St. Louis. Larry credits Paula with his renewed passion for the Lord and considers her to be one of the greatest blessings heaven ever bestowed on him.

Then in January 1992, about four years into their happy marriage, Larry woke up to a heart attack. Paula rushed him to the hospital and an x-ray discovered a spot on his lung—cancer.

Doctors worked on his heart first and then took out half of his lung. He was hospitalized for three and half weeks and returned to work a month later.

Three years passed. At a routine check-up Larry discovered his cancer had returned, this time in a lymph node in his chest. Extensive chemotherapy and radiation forced him to retire at age fifty-one, which made him feel "like not much of a man." He joined the Cancer Support Group of St. Louis and he and Paula together joined the Cancer Wellness Center, which they describe as "a godsend." When he heard I was to be in St. Louis to autograph my new book *The Worth of a Man*, he came to the bookstore and we met. He identified with my story, picked up a copy of the book, and later told me it changed his whole attitude. He, too, had suffered for years by connecting his worth with his ability to work. How freeing and wonderful to learn that God's valuation of him didn't vary depending on what he was able to do! The realization came just in time, for new challenges loomed on the horizon.

In 1996 Larry discovered the cancer had returned for a third time, now in the lymph nodes in his neck. While he endured four more months of chemo, his elderly father died at age eighty-five. "I was glad that he did not know what was happening in my life; I wanted him to be at peace in his latter years," Larry said.

In 1997 he learned that the chemo did not eradicate all his cancer. Doctors wanted to wait four months to decide what to do, and by the time he got a CT scan, the tumor had doubled in size. Many doctors did not want to do surgery because the growth had wrapped itself around a cluster of nerves; they feared an operation could cause paralysis or death. Larry had the tumor removed anyway and came home the following day, only to return to the hospital the next day with pneumonia; he was running a temperature of 102 and had difficulty breathing. Shortly thereafter he discovered he had developed diabetes.

To complicate matters further, while Larry was in the hospital, Paula was rushed to the emergency room where she discovered she needed gall bladder surgery. She chose to delay the operation until Larry returned from the hospital. The day before her surgery, Larry decided to help by going to the store for groceries. But after returning home he told Paula to call 911; he thought he was having a mild heart attack. Hospital tests confirmed he had suffered an angina attack and needed to see a cardiologist.

We wanted to encourage the Talleys through all this turmoil and on July 30, 1997, tried to give them a call. They weren't home so we left a message on their answering machine that said, "Where are you? We are worried and it is a sin to worry. Please don't make us sin. Call us." The next day Larry left *us* a message: "This is God. Don't worry."

Despite his deteriorating health, Larry manages to joke. And he has some advice for others who, like him, struggle with bodies that don't work as well as they'd like. He's not a preacher, but you'd be wise to take note of his words.

"God made each of us unique and different and in that difference we all need our own time to mourn the loss of whatever cancer has done to our bodies and minds," he says. "We each will be different in how we handle our pain, discouragement, the loss of being whole. We will be different in the time it takes to gather the strength to come back and be a part of the world again. Each will be different in how they handle the thought of death. So when some well-meaning person tells us to get over it and get on with life, tell them (in a nice way) to stuff it. You'll get on with life in your own time, not theirs."

Larry has another piece of advice for those who are suffering: don't hesitate to tell your friends and relatives about the things that bother you. "After all," he says, "God commands us to walk in the light." Larry also says he doesn't need people so much to tell him what to do as he needs them to be his friends and to walk alongside him in loving support. And everyone can do that.

15

THANK GOD FOR THE TRIALS!

We got a hint about the character of Jim Arnoldi about three years ago when he first contacted the Outreach of Hope. Although he had been wrestling for five years with his own difficult cancer (and already by that time had undergone nine major surgeries), he wrote, "I'm enclosing a check . . . and am praying that you will touch many lives with your efforts." We know for certain that he touched our lives, and I think he'll touch yours, too.

No wife wants to hear the surgeon say her husband is in critical condition in the Intensive Care Unit, but Carole Arnoldi has heard the words so often she says they now "almost seem a matter of routine." That's because her husband, Jim, has undergone eighteen major surgeries since his first one on February 12, 1990. "We face death in a real way, over and over," Carole says. "I often feel like death is knocking on our door."

Jim heard the first rapping in November of 1989 when the acute abdominal pains began. A prescribed drug had no effect and Jim's pain grew worse. By February 12 Jim found himself in the hospital facing his first surgery. Doctors discovered that a growing tumor about the size of a Nerf football had burst, spreading diseased tissue throughout Jim's abdomen. It took two months to determine the tumor was malignant. The dreaded result came only after the Armed Forces Pathological Institute in Washington, D.C., identified it as a very rare cancer known as Leiomyosarcoma. This form of cancer doesn't respond to radiation therapy or chemotherapy; the only treatment is surgical removal of the tumors.

The Arnoldis soon learned that patients with this disease have an average life expectancy of three years (the record was seven years). Two "second opinions" later, Jim had to accept that more surgeries were on his horizon. "It's probably good we didn't know how difficult the future was to be," he says.

The next few years brought several surgeries in Jim's small bowel. In 1993 doctors found cancer on Jim's liver and his surgeon recommended his next operation be performed at Mount Sinai Hospital in New York. That surgery uncovered approximately *fifty* tumors, ten of which lay on the liver, and doctors decided to try a chemo treatment used in other types of cancer. To say it didn't work vastly understates the truth. Jim promptly went into a coma and the platinum in the deadly solution shut down his kidneys. From that time on he's endured a kidney dialysis routine of three hours, three times a week. His cancer makes him ineligible for a transplant.

A CT scan in September 1997 revealed that the right lobe of Jim's liver is now totally covered with cancer; recurrent tumors lie in Jim's abdomen and behind the stomach; and new tumors lie in the left lung. In October Jim endured his eighteenth major surgery— and for the first time, doctors were unable to remove all the cancer they found. The chief surgeon at Emory University Hospital in Atlanta looked Jim in the eye and said, "Are you prepared that this may be the beginning of the end?" He then suggested Jim would "probably start going downhill in three to six months"; unfortunately, the prognosis seems accurate. Between Thanksgiving 1997 and January 1998, Jim entered the hospital eight times for various ailments, including internal bleeding (origin unknown). In addition, he suffers such pain on the bottom of his heels—a side effect of kidney dialysis—that he often has difficulty walking.

All this leads Jim to believe that the end may very well be approaching. But he's grateful that "the Lord has given me all this to time to prepare and get ready. Heaven's not a bad place to go to—although I'd really rather have the Rapture take place first so all of us can go at the same time!"

Jim speaks with such steadiness of voice and so often sprinkles his conversation with humor that it's hard to imagine the pain and suffering he has endured in the last nine years. Of course, it wasn't always this way.

"When I lay in the hospital after that initial surgery, waiting for the diagnosis that was to change my life," he says, "my first reaction was 'Why me?' I began to suggest to God there were many others who deserved this fate more than I! I was so sure he had the wrong person. There must be some mistake! Surely, the final, authoritative report would say NEGATIVE. Not malignant. But that wasn't to be. The report said positive: malignant. Something I never wanted to hear."

At some point down the road, however, Jim stopped asking "Why me?" and began asking "Why NOT me?" He saw that although he had been a believer all his life, he wasn't where he needed to be spiritually. In short, he hadn't been depending on God. And he believes the Lord used his illness to get his attention.

"Thank God for the trials!" he says today. "How would we grow without the sifting and shaping of God's hand in our lives? How would we learn? How would we ever experience the power of his Presence, if we didn't get into the valleys? I know I learned more in the valleys than I ever did on the mountain tops.

"Although I can have hope for better health or a successful operation, what I need to rest in is the promise that God will sustain me in all circumstances and provide me a residence in his Presence, no matter what. I think most of us spend too much time seeking a way *out* of a situation, rather than pleading with God for a way *through* it. Since cancer took hold of me, I found that praying for acceptance is far more comforting in the long haul. If we believe that God is Sovereign, and that all things first pass through his fingers, then do we stand firm in our faith if we suggest God 'got the wrong guy' when trials befall us? We can gain so much from our difficulties that we shouldn't waste time looking for a way out. Haven't we heard so many say, after much suffering, 'I've never felt so close to the Lord' or 'My spiritual life has grown amazingly'?"

Jim insists that cancer has provided him the opportunity of a lifetime to grow in a way he might never have otherwise known.

He says he didn't find his purpose for living until he thought about dying. Then it occurred to him that he had no place to run to and no one to lean on. But on his back, looking up, Jim discovered that God was watching and waiting for his response.

"Sometimes I think we get the best view of Christ and his Presence when we are lying on our back," he says. "That's when I began to see. God was in my own shadow before he moved me aside so that his Presence was in full view. It was then that I realized there was only One to go to, One to whom I could turn. I found that I could endure anything, as long as I depended on Christ for *everything*. Yielding to him opens the door to a new world, a world where he becomes the focus. What a wonderful distraction that is from the pain and suffering that accompanies serious illness!"

Distraction, yes; but release? No.

"Do I struggle?" Jim asks. "Definitely! Almost nine years of battling cancer takes a toll on a family. Life changes for all concerned, not just the patient. Sometimes I think the kidney failure is the worst, in terms of daily living. Three dialysis treatments a week seriously hampers life in our home. As a patient, you tend to feel washed out each time. So, most times, I can't fully participate in family activities. That doesn't make it very nice for the rest of the family.

"Vacations are extremely difficult. Night activities are nonexistent. Weekends away are nearly impossible. Chris, my thirteen-year-old son, probably feels this the most. He has a dad who just can't do things with him as much as he'd like. Carol, my wife, has become a care giver. My twenty-two-year-old has to continually do jobs around the house that I can't do myself. Tina, my twenty-five-year-old, is at graduate school, always wondering with the rest: 'What next?' I struggle most with watching my family struggle!"

Carole agrees with her husband. "Our family suffers in many ways," she says. "Our twenty-five-year-old daughter went back to graduate school recently, following another disappointing CT scan report. More tumors, spread further! Will she see her father again? How long will he be here for her? How many times following a holiday has she left home, with the real possibility that she won't see him again? Our twenty-two-year-old son lives at home. How often has he been disappointed that his dad couldn't do things with him? Our eighth grader, Chris, was in kindergarten when Jim was first diagnosed. How many times has he gone to school, with Jim in for surgery, wondering if he would have a dad when he got home? I find life difficult. There is a sick world and a well one. It's hard for the well to understand the day-to-day lives of the sick and their families."

Beyond that, Jim worries that people tend to look at the patient and not the patient's family. While Carole gets bombarded with "How's your husband?" few people through the years have asked her, "How are *you* doing?" It simply is not easy living day after day in a home where death camps just outside the door.

That's why Jim believes it is important to discuss openly the realities and potential outcomes of his disease. He deemed it especially crucial to share with Chris his beliefs about God's providence, Jesus' sacrifice for us, and the great promise of salvation and eternal life. For Jim, a vital relationship with Jesus Christ is the ultimate bottom line.

Because Jim's ultimate concern is a person's connection to God, his conversations with non-Christian friends sometimes cause him great personal pain. For his own part, "The more I look full into Jesus' face, the more tolerable my state is. It's only when I get sidetracked and waver in my commitment that I show signs of weakening. It is only through submission that I begin to feel his strength in me to overcome my present condition. He has chosen to grant me an extension on life beyond what anyone expected. I sure have much to rejoice about, even though the battle continues. That it continues at all certainly borders on the miraculous."

16

WHEN STRUGGLES COME, BLESSINGS FOLLOW

Bob and Ethel Rose have been such an encouragement to us at the Outreach of Hope that we featured them in a 1997 article in our ministry's publication The Encourager. *Under the headline, "Surviving with Cancer—Finding the Blessings," Bob and Ethel described the difference between surviving* from *the disease and surviving* with *it.*

We believe so strongly in their message that we wanted to give them an opportunity to address a larger audience. We think you'll be blessed, as we have, with their unique perspective on suffering.

Ethel Rose planned to celebrate her birthday on November 7, 1989, by meeting her mother and sister for lunch. But first she wanted to accompany her husband, Robert, to his doctor's appointment where he expected to be treated for hemorrhoids. But things didn't turn out as planned.

As Ethel waited outside the examination room, Bob endured the embarrassing and painful exam. Without warning, the doctor suddenly said, "Well, there's no two ways about it. You've got cancer. I'm going to go ahead and do a biopsy. Put your clothes back on and meet me in the office and we'll talk about it."

A verse immediately popped into Bob's mind: "It is appointed unto man once to die." While reeling from the doctor's abrupt announcement, he still found great comfort in knowing he would die only once and then be in God's presence. He quickly dressed and retrieved his wife, telling her nothing, then the two of them went to the doctor's office. The doctor soon entered the room carrying a thick medical book, pointed to a picture of a diseased colon, bluntly said "This is cancer," and proceeded to tell the Roses that Bob had it. Immediate surgery was required.

The news was made harder by a secret Bob and Ethel shared: Chad, their youngest son and a senior in high school, was out of control, drinking heavily and partying. Later they also discovered he was addicted to drugs, including LSD and marijuana.

"Here was this loving, accelerated student—athletic, popular, and handsome—who had been strong in the Lord, sharing his faith with others . . . now becoming a person we didn't know," Ethel recalls. For four years Chad had led team prayers on the high school football team, starting a tradition that remains to this day.

On the day of Bob's surgery, family and friends started showing up at the hospital at the crack of dawn to pray and support the Roses; so many came that the hospital put them in a conference room. The surgery seemed to go well but a few days later as a surgeon examined Bob, a nurse knocked at the door and asked to speak to the doctor. Twice he told her he was busy, but finally she whispered softly from the door, "I need to talk to you." He left and returned moments later, wearing a concerned look. "Robert," he said, "I'm sorry, but your pathology report came back and it shows a microscopic tumor has been cut. You have to have surgery immediately."

A second opinion confirmed the awful diagnosis and Bob learned that because the tumor had been cut it would spread—and even with surgery and radical chemo, he had perhaps six months to live. When Ethel heard the prognosis, she felt faint and sick to her stomach . She sat on a step stool in the room, put her head between her knees, and tried to get herself together. "As we left the office all I wanted to do was to hold Robert and never let him go," she said. "I loved him so much that I wasn't prepared to lose him." Bob and Ethel immediately headed for their family practitioner, a good friend, and sat in one of his rooms for three hours, crying and praying and trying to decide what to do.

Later that day Bob checked into the hospital and underwent radical abdominal surgery that resulted in a permanent colostomy. Following a time of recuperation, Bob began a series of radiation treatments. Naturally it was a difficult time, but "as a couple we continued to draw closer together," Ethel said, "praying and sharing with each other what we were thinking and feeling—even to the point of discussing what I should do if he were to die. I didn't want to think about it, but we had to discuss it." These discussions would be the catalyst for the later formation of a cancer support group.

More surgeries followed. In 1991 Bob spent New Year's in the emergency room with an appendix ready to burst. Ethel began asking herself, "How is he going to get through this? There seems to be no end to any of it." Bob also recognized the hardship. "I don't mean to belittle the reality of trusting God, because I know he is trustworthy, but when you are outside the operating room and give your spouse that last kiss good-bye, reality sets in," he says. "Those are dark hours."

M*eanwhile, Bob and Ethel didn't feel as if they could tell anyone about their problems with Chad. Ethel didn't want anyone to know how terrible things really were and wondered, If people knew, what would they say about us? What have we done wrong? The Roses watched their son sink deeper into the world of addiction, complete with frightening and bizarre behavior.*

"I remember the nights Robert and I would sit on the sofa, holding each other and crying and pleading for God to intervene," Ethel said. "We'd say, 'Make it stop! Make it stop!'"

On March 17, 1991, both Bob and Ethel independently were praying that God would bring things to a head with Chad. On that day their son overdosed on LSD. Bob came home from Sunday services to find him curled up in a ball on his bed, terrified and begging for help. It turned out that while on the way to a friend's house Chad had a vision of God, who looked directly at him and angrily shook his head NO. The image frightened Chad so badly he opened his car window and chucked all his drug paraphernalia outside.

His parents placed him in a recovery hospital where they were told Chad would never again be a normal, functioning person. When their insurance money almost ran out, they moved him to another facility about two hours away and visited him five to six times a week during his month-long stay. At that point Bob and Ethel finally told the church about their struggle, and to their great relief the congregation rallied around them. Somebody in their church paid for the whole treatment and wouldn't let them repay a dime.

Chad returned home a renewed young man. He joined Alcoholics Anonymous and stayed off drugs and alcohol from then on. He even began witnessing in seedy downtown areas that most people wouldn't even visit.

One day when Bob was flying to Southern California, a scruffy-looking young man came walking down the aisle. "I was hoping he wasn't going to sit next to me," Bob confesses. "He had purple hair and spikes on his wrist and boots, black clothes, and a huge cross hanging from his neck. Of all the places on that airplane to sit, he sat next to me—and if you think I was happy about that, you've got another thing coming. But you see, God had a plan. Chad plucked him from a literal gutter one evening and had led this young man to Christ, walking him away from drugs and alcohol."

Ethel attended her own recovery meetings where she learned some hard and painful truths about herself. "But I knew I had to change, even though I would fight the truth," she says. "I'm still having to work at the changes God wants for me. Changes don't come easy. We found ourselves becoming open and transparent, sharing our struggles and our hopes. We discovered there were other people just like us."

Bob and Ethel soon formed a Hope In Christ Cancer Support Group with two other couples from their church. While it isn't a Bible study, they often share Christ in their meetings. They talk about every area of their lives—work, finances, sex, relationships, marriages. An average of sixteen to twenty currently attend each week; in five years the group has lost twenty-two members to cancer. Bob and Ethel consider this group their ministry and calling, their "divine niche" in life.

"Many people think being involved with suffering and dying people is the most depressing and demoralizing thing," Bob says, "but it has brought indescribable blessing to Ethel and me. Yes, we cry at times, but we laugh as much as we cry—sometimes more than we cry."

What many people fear, Bob and Ethel Rose have come to call "blessings." They started looking for and counting those blessings in September 1990 when they took a trip to Europe, "a trip I wasn't supposed to be alive to take," Bob says. "When we recognized the significance of that, we started to notice the blessings. Through this process we have learned that when struggles come, blessings follow. So when things look bad, we look at each other and ask, 'I wonder how God is going to bless us this time?' We have come to realize that God has been with us—blessing us—since the beginning. It took us awhile to recognize some of the blessings, but they have been there all along."

More opportunities for "blessings" came in the years 1992 to 1994 when Bob endured seven more surgeries, almost lost his arm in a car accident, and nearly died from an infection. In 1993 he dragged his older son, Robert, "kicking and screaming" to the Promise Keepers gathering in Boulder, Colorado. His son had fallen away from the faith because he couldn't understand why God would allow his father to endure so many trials. But when he arrived at the stadium and looked around, he said, "Dad, this is the Jesus Super Bowl. This is like nothing I've ever seen in my life. This is the Jesus Super Bowl. Just look at these men!" Robert sat by his father for two days and did nothing but cry. God touched him there and revived his faith.

Two years before this Chad began attending a private college and continued getting his life together. He was doing well in school and began to develop his love for writing poetry. He had decided he wanted to teach special education kids. But on August 8, 1995, Bob and Ethel awoke at 1:20 A.M. to a loud knock at their door.

A man identified himself as the Sacramento County Coroner and asked if they were the parents of Chad Gerald Rose. He was sorry to tell them that twenty-three-year-old Chad had died that evening while at work. Ethel froze while Bob fell to the floor, calling out to God. They learned that night as Chad worked at an ice cream shop he suddenly collapsed behind the counter; the coroner said he was dead before he hit the floor. Cause of death was never firmly established, but toxicological reports showed Chad was still "clean" from drugs and alcohol.

Even in this tragedy, however, God provided a blessing. The coroner could tell the Roses were a Christian couple and as he prepared to leave, he asked to pray with them. In months to come, four people influenced by Chad's death came to Christ.

Still, "There are not words that can express the pain we all experienced at that time," Ethel said. "As a parent, we don't expect to bury our children. To this day we are still healing from the loss of Chad."

About four months later Ethel's eighty-eight-year-old dad came to live with the Roses. He was dying of cancer but would not talk about Chad's death. For years Ethel had prayed for her dad's salvation without apparent effect. But during his last days he accepted the Lord and Bob and Ethel began to witness a remarkable transformation. He witnessed to everyone who came to see him, telling them they should be reconciled to God. Ethel repeatedly told him they would all be with Chad again in heaven. When she heard him say, "Let's pray!" and saw his tears fall as she described heaven, her heart nearly exploded. Her father died two weeks later, at his own request dressed in Chad's clothes, because he said he was going to be with Chad and wanted to be ready to see his grandson.

Such are the blessings the Roses have come to expect. Of course, they wouldn't want to go through these events again! "But without these things happening," Ethel says, "I wouldn't know that Jesus is real and that he wants to restore and mend broken lives and broken hearts. God wants to heal us spiritually first and does not always choose to heal us physically."

"Our family still cries a lot because we miss our son and our other departed loved ones," Bob adds, "but we don't weep as those without hope in Jesus Christ."

These days Bob has checkups every six months and doctors continue to cut precancerous growths from his body. A recent CT scan found no signs of cancer and Bob and Ethel both believe God has done another miracle in their lives.

Yet another blessing. And Bob and Ethel just keep counting.

17

THE MESSAGE OF THE TRIPLE RAINBOW

In 1953 a girl named Rachel was born to a Mennonite family in Mountain Lake, Minnesota. Rachel and her four brothers grew up on a farm where a strong work ethic ruled. Early on Rachel displayed a vibrant love for life and she approached the world with the awe and insight of an artist.

Steve Earll met Rachel while he was teaching a karate class at her college. Her determination attracted him and he immediately labeled her a fighter. "Little did I know how much that would be a theme in our lives," he says.

"I remember the moment I fell in love with Rachel," says Steve Earll. "During a karate class I chose her to help demonstrate a technique. I grabbed her from behind in a choke hold and then taught her how to throw me. The throw left the back of the attacker exposed and the follow-up technique was to be a kick to the kidneys. After several slow motion throws, I told her to throw me using full power. Rachel snapped into a beautiful throw, but in her excitement failed to control her kick to my kidneys. I lay on the mat in severe pain, trying not to pass out—while Rachel and the rest of the class gathered around me, laughing uncontrollably. I realized that any woman who could handle me like that was worth loving."

The pair dated for more than two years. Outside of class she worked with troubled youth, while he toiled as a substance abuse therapist. They were married in April 1977.

In 1981 when Rachel became pregnant, she felt strongly that something was "wrong" with the baby and prayed earnestly until the conviction stopped. When Emily was born, it was discovered the umbilical cord had been wrapped around her thigh. At some point the cord uncoiled, saving Emily's leg. Rachel often told this story to Emily as a reminder that she was "a miracle baby."

In August 1984 Kaylee was born. Three months later on a November afternoon Rachel noticed her daughter had stopped breathing. She rushed Kaylee to the hospital, where the baby was diagnosed with apnea. For the next ten months Kaylee was connected to a heart monitor that sounded an alarm each time her heart rate or breathing fell below certain levels. On an average night, the alarm sounded seven to thirteen times. In time Kaylee grew out of her condition and Rachel reminded her often of her own "miracle baby" story.

One night Rachel and Steve decided to shop for an hour before going to a movie. They were walking up a flight of stairs in a sporting goods store when a forty-five pound basketball backboard fell from an upper level, striking Rachel on the head. The blow instantly transformed Rachel emotionally from a thirty-year-old woman to a ten-year-old child.

"Rachel lost all sense of who she was," Steve recalls. "She could no longer remember directions, how to cook, or how to comparison shop. She could not trust her memory. Tasks that had been easy for her were now impossible."

The accident also damaged Rachel's back, making it difficult for her to pick up or carry her children. A two-year rehabilitation process ensued in which she learned her mental limits—and then pushed for more. The family eventually adjusted to her head injury and life became "normal" again.

"Rachel and I also had the mistaken sense that we had finished our life quota of hardship," Steve says.

In 1991 Rachel discovered some lumps in her right breast; tests confirmed they were cancerous. Soon chemotherapy and a mastectomy were scheduled. By this time Emily and Kaylee were nine and six, respectively, and their concerns came out in caring and cute ways. Emily once approached Rachel, pulled up her shirt, and said,

"Mommy, aren't little girls' boobies cute?" A confused Rachel said yes, they were. "Just think, Mommy, you are going to look just like this!" Emily exclaimed.

Chemo was difficult. Rachel lost all her hair and rather than use wigs, she started wearing scarves of beautiful fabric, tying them in attractive ways and pairing them with hats. Women at church started to ask Rachel how to create such ensembles. So one Sunday a month the women of the church wore hats and scarves to show their support for Rachel.

Treatments came once a month for six months, while blood tests were taken every three months. "It was like going before a judge four times a year to be told if we were going to be allowed to live or not," Steve said.

Rachel stayed "clean" for two years, then in the spring of 1994 a CT scan showed a shadow of cancer behind Rachel's breast-bone, near the arteries and nerves by the heart. The area was inoperable and radiation not a possibility; stem cell replacement was judged the only possible treatment. Doctors said a successful procedure would gain Rachel one to three years of life, but they gave her only a ten percent possibility of a cure.

It was time for Rachel the fighter to start swinging again. She fasted, tried a vegetarian diet, then began treatments once more. Although she was very sick, she insisted on going to church, sometimes only to sit in the reception hall for thirty minutes so she could talk to friends. "She fought cancer with dignity," Steve said.

Once during her stem cell replacement therapy, she described a visit by what she believed to be an angel sitting beside her. Another time she had a vivid vision of Jesus in which she said to him, "If you touch me, I will be healed." In her vision, Christ not only touched her, he reached out and hugged her. The vision became a source of strength and comfort for the rest of her life.

There were also times of humor. One night Steve set up a cot in her room so he could stay through the night and, she asked what he was doing. "I'm sleeping here tonight," he replied. And in a sincere, little girl voice she asked, "Does your mother know?"

Gradually Rachel fought her way back to health. Weekly tests gave way to monthly tests, then to tests every three months. Two years passed. But in the spring of 1997, Rachel began to suffer from allergies. Eventually her allergies gave way to a pervasive cold, then bronchitis. At the hospital doctors removed more than one liter of fluid from her lungs; two weeks later another liter of fluid came out. An echocardiogram revealed fluid around Rachel's heart, and the oncologist said that could mean only one thing: cancer. Rachel would die.

Rachel was admitted to the hospital, where she continued to talk to her girls about everyday things—school, boys, sports. "The interchanges were an example of deep need and pure love," Steve recalls. "No one was denying the truth. Death was to be treated as a moment in time and everything up to that moment was life. Rachel and the girls were celebrating their relationship."

Late one evening during some routine tests, Rachel's blood oxygen level dropped rapidly to dangerous levels. The girls were sent home while hospital staff began emergency procedures. Rachel was placed on oxygen and transported to the coronary intensive care unit. Steve remained with her all night, closely watching the myriad graphs, numbers, and sounds that measure life.

The next day before surgery, Emily, Kaylee, Steve, and Rachel said good-bye to each other and prayed. They knew it might be their last time together. Then Rachel left for surgery as church members surrounded the family.

Minutes became hours. When surgeons reemerged from the operating room, they bore grim news: Rachel's lungs and heart were filled with cancer. All hope of a miracle or chemo treatment disappeared. Death could occur at any time.

For twenty-four hours a sedated Rachel depended on a respirator, while her husband sat listening to the rhythm of a machine that blew air into her lungs like a balloon. Doctors said they would keep Rachel on the respirator for another day, no more. Steve went home to shower, change clothes, and phone family members with the devastating news. But by the time he returned to the hospital, a new medical team had succeeded at removing Rachel from the machine—the first of many miracles.

Rachel remained in critical condition and family members began arriving from the Midwest to say their good-byes. Steve remained at the hospital day and night. "I could not bring myself to leave," he said. "I spent my nights quietly, trying to memorize every move, every breath, the way that she looked, every word spoken."

On July 4 Rachel took a turn for the worse and a new physician announced coldly that Rachel had only two hours to live unless she chose to return to the respirator. That meant she would have to be sedated and might never come off the machine. Rachel refused that option and used the time to talk to her children and husband. Once again the family gathered at her bed in prayer, expressed their love for each other, and said their good-byes. Then Rachel slept.

In the afternoon she woke up, looked at Steve with determination in her eyes, and asked, "What if I don't die?" Again in the evening she awoke, smiled at her husband and declared, "I knew I wasn't going to die!"

Rachel had started to fight. And conventional medical wisdom had to be adjusted. Simply put, Rachel refused to die.

Each day when the doctor came in, Rachel asked questions about her condition. Upon hearing the medical facts, she got angry. When she got angry, she began to fight. And when she fought, her vitals began to rise and everyone knew she wasn't going to die any time soon.

Rachel also got angry with her family. Many of them tried to give her permission to die instead of hanging on and suffering, but Rachel wouldn't hear of it. Eventually she demanded that Steve tell everyone to quit talking about dying, angels, and visions. She didn't feel like going anywhere, much less dying.

Still, doctors insisted death was imminent. And since she was dying, they decided she could eat anything she wanted. She ordered breakfast but was so weak she could barely hold a fork. When Steve moved to help feed her, she instantly gave him a look that said, "Back off!" Rachel was not only going to eat, she was going to feed herself!

Over time Rachel became stronger and began to request that she be allowed to go home. One major problem: it looked as if only a mdeical setting could provide the oxygen system she needed to survive.

At the end of the second week Rachel's doctor was talking about sending her to a nursing home hospice program. This depressed Rachel and she wrestled with God over why she must die when her girls were so young. She accepted that God was sovereign and would take care of her husband and her girls, but it was too hard to accept that God wanted her to die in a unknown unit away from home. Rachel knew that if she was transferred to a nursing home, she would give up.

Then another miracle occurred. A church friend stepped in, a nursing supervisor for a home-based hospice care program. She arranged for the needed oxygen to be supplied at the Earll home. Rachel and Steve's bedroom was quickly converted into a comfortable care room, complete with hospital bed and other needed equipment.

Emily and Kaylee dived into her care. They helped with bathing chores, bed changing, and all the comfort needs of their mom. They spent hours talking and reading to her. Many times they would crawl up in to her bed either to hold or to be held by her. As Rachel became weaker and more childlike, their roles reversed and the girls became the comforting parents to Rachel. Both Kaylee and Emily displayed the courage they had learned from their mother.

Rachel regained remarkable energy by returning home. She insisted on seeing everyone who came to visit until she was beyond exhaustion. Church friends put together two song services with electric keyboard and bass guitar set up in the bedroom. As many as fifteen people crammed into the room for these sessions. Rachel glowed as she listened or sang through her oxygen mask.

During this time Rachel also planned her own funeral service. She met with her pastor concerning all aspects of the service and also discussed the music, picking out favorite songs. She intended her service to be a celebration, upbeat and focused on God. She said she wanted people dancing in the aisles.

Rachel often said that she did not know how to die. Yet she wanted to die in Steve's arms because she knew how much he loved her. "He is such a part of me and I am so much a part of him," she told Steve's sister, Jean. "If you took out my heart it would belong to Steve. It's hard to separate that kind of closeness. God has truly made us one."

Rachel lived at home for more than five weeks and during that time received over two hundred visitors. During the first several weeks she did so well that many people started to believe that perhaps there had been a miracle and God had healed her. But it was not to be.

Rachel was conscious for the last time on a Thursday morning. By that time she had become like a child and she asked Steve how to get to heaven. He read the passage of salvation from John 3:16 and she said she had accepted Christ. He then read about heaven from Revelation 21. He woke up the girls to be with their mother and announced they were going to pray. Steve didn't think Rachel could pray, but before he could begin, she prayed a beautiful prayer for the blessing of each member of her family. Minutes later, she became disoriented, went to sleep, and lapsed into a coma that continued until the next Monday.

Death came late Monday afternoon. She passed quietly, with her family around her, just as she had wished.

Shortly before her death, Rachel told her girls that if God would allow it, she would find a way to let them know she was happy in heaven.

She always loved rainbows, and less than an hour after she died, a triple rainbow appeared in the sky directly over the Earll home. Family and friends gathered in the middle of the street, marveling and taking photos of the multicolored sky. No one could remember seeing a triple rainbow before that day. And across town, a family friend who also saw the rainbows—but who had not heard of Rachel's death—said to Steve, "That must be Rachel!"

18

I KNOW THAT
MY REDEEMER LIVES

Kari Lundberg has suffered intensely for more than thirty years with
an exotic range of ailments. Yet she insists the issue is not WHY we
suffer. Her own constant, unrelenting pain lets her know she was never
singled out for suffering; she believes it is simply part of being human.

"In the Western world we feel offended at the fact that we suffer,"
she says. "We think, God surely has an obligation to see to it that nothing nasty befalls me! And our constant wail is, 'Why me?' In my own
decades of intense pain and suffering, I have found that my only satis-
faction is found in the words of Job 19:25 (NASB)—"And as for me, I
know that my Redeemer lives"

Getting to that assurance, however, has taken Kari many long
nights of weeping, groaning, and utter despair. And those nights began
early in her life.

I was introduced to suffering the day I was born. It was the
beginning of the German occupation of our small country during
World War II, and the city of Oslo, Norway, was in total blackout. A pristine white snow was falling that night, and so were the
bombs of Germany's Luftwaffe.

I spent the first five years of my life in constant fear and
poverty. Those daily hours of massive bombing and destruction
left deep impressions on me that last till this day. Every night we
went to bed with our clothes on. We knew that within a couple
of hours we would have to get up and crawl into the "safety" of the
bomb shelter under our apartment building. It was dark in this
space, and the low ceiling prevented us from standing up. Once

in awhile someone would light a candle to dimly illuminate the space and we all rejoiced in this small blessing.

My family lacked adequate food, medicine, and decent shelter, and at age four I came down with tuberculosis. I, in turn, gave the disease to my mother. I was sent to one sanatorium, my mother to another, and for months we were thus separated. The pain of separation was far worse than the illness. I still remember the room of twenty beds in which I was confined.

Yet even at this young age I had been introduced to the faith of my parents. I was taught that no matter our circumstances, Christ himself would sustain us. We may find ourselves in desperate circumstances, but God will provide the means by which we will ultimately be redeemed.

After my stay at the sanatorium, I went to live with my maternal grandmother. Her unfailing faith in God and the power of prayer influenced me greatly. At age forty-two she was left a widow for the second time, and by herself she had reared seven children under the age of fourteen. I still remember sitting on the floor outside her bedroom in the morning, listening to her prayers. She prayed aloud and mentioned every name in her extended family. Whenever my name came up, I felt a tremendous presence of God. I knew that no matter what happened to me, my Redeemer lives.

Then 1945 came and the war finally ended. I will never forget the day our King Haakon the Seventh and his family returned. To see our own flag fly after six years of occupation brought not only tears of national pride, but also provided a spiritual lesson: There will be a day of redemption!

At last we were free to attend the house of worship of our own choosing. During the war we met in private homes, always in fear for our lives. We sang the hymns in hushed tones and preached the sermons in voices barely above a whisper. Now we could gather openly and raise our voices in a collective shout of praise!

I was active in The Salvation Army, which strongly supports the equality of men and women in the ministry. I had received my call to ministry and life was going well for me. I graduated early from college and was teaching school in Norway when a call came from a Norwegian-speaking church in Brooklyn. I quickly left for the United States to become an assistant minister and God richly blessed my ministry in this new land. After a couple of years, I met Ake Lundberg, the man who would become my life-long partner, husband, lover, and friend. God soon blessed us with a son and life could not have been better.

Then events occurred which altered our lives forever.

One morning I got up to get our baby ready for the day. I bent over the crib to pick up Sven—and let out a scream. I had ruptured a disc and my back locked up into excruciating pain. During a five-hour surgery to correct the damage, doctors discovered I suffered from a degenerative disc disease. The pain was unbearable and my prognosis discouraging. For many weeks I lay flat on my back in the hospital.

Then one morning I woke up with an excruciating headache, accompanied by severe vomiting. Next diagnosis: encephalitis and spinal meningitis. Immediately I was sent to an isolation room and quickly slipped into a coma.

"Your wife will die soon," doctors told Ake. "Go home and prepare the funeral."

But God had other plans. Our Redeemer still lives!

On the fourth day of my coma, students and staff of the seminary we attended called for an all-night prayer vigil. They began praying at eleven in the evening and continued until eleven the following morning. Fifteen minutes after they concluded their prayers, I sat up in bed and asked for breakfast—as if nothing had happened! Two days later I walked out of the hospital under my own power. Hospital staff lined the hallway and applauded as I left. Even my unbelieving doctor said this was a medical impossibility; a Higher Power must have been at work.

Yet although my life had been spared, my health had taken a heavy blow. My condition forced us to leave the ministry and for six weeks our little family of three lived in a ten-by-ten-foot room provided by some dear friends. It was the darkest of times.

Some time later we were finally able to settle into our own home and my husband found new work. Within a year Ake got a phone call from Sherwood Wirt, the editor of *Decision* magazine, and soon he was invited to join the Billy Graham team as its photographer. We moved to Minneapolis, Minnesota, and thought, *Finally! Now life is on an even keel.*

We were wrong.

A year after we moved I needed another back surgery; three more quickly followed. I spent most of my time either in the hospital or in bed at home, in utter agony. Then came several other surgeries unrelated to my back.

Sadly, callous Christians intensified our suffering by telling us, "You are suffering because you have too little faith," or "There must be hidden sin in your lives; otherwise you would be healed." The darkness of the night almost consumed me and I had nothing in my hands with which to fight back.

Except faith in my Redeemer! I believed God is love, and although my faith may have wobbled, it did not fall down. God is the giver of all good gifts, and I knew he does not zap someone for lack of something better to do. I realized that in this fallen world we get sick, we lose loved ones, and we suffer emotionally. Thank God this world is not all there is!

Since those difficult days I have been diagnosed with both fibromyalgia and chronic fatigue syndrome. To date, I have endured eight back surgeries, seven other surgeries, multiple kidney failures, and thirty years of debilitating, chronic pain. I have been hospitalized for five years of our thirty-four-year marriage and not a day goes by that I do not have pain.

Yet God has been faithful. He has allowed me to see our son grow into adulthood. In the midst of so much suffering, Sven's own faith has grown into great maturity. My marriage has always been close and by the grace of God Ake and I are now more deeply in love than ever.

My ministry has shifted to working one-to-one with people going through life changes. The suffering has enabled me to walk with others who are just starting out on their own spiritual journeys.

I have also learned that the medical profession is often either untrained or unwilling to deal with people in chronic pain. I have been called almost every name in the book, just because I would ask for medicine to give me a few moments of relief. My current doctor (may his name be blessed!) has spent most of his medical career treating those of us with unrelenting, excruciating, debilitating pain, and I now have a narcotics pump delivery system implanted in my body which continually drips a painkiller directly into my spine—and for the first time in thirty years, most of my back pain is gone!

Yet I must still deal with the muscle and joint pain resulting from fibromyalgia and arthritis, and kidney damage leaves me with low blood pressure and morning faintness. In addition, the chronic fatigue syndrome leaves me exhausted and mentally tired most of the time.

Still, I don't think that's the worst of it. In this culture, the chronically ill are often forced to live a life of anonymity and isolation. The healthy often think, *Hey, you get sick, you fix it, and you move on.* Rare is the person who sticks around someone with a chronic illness—and the aloneness is much worse than the illness itself. Many a time I was hospitalized for months, yet never received a single visit from anyone belonging to my church.

Our culture also discourages us from talking about suffering and illness. It's taboo. I have listened to endless tales of people's boring jobs and their wonderful grandchildren (to the point of nausea), but if I dared to mention what my life has been like, I have been greeted with dead silence and a heavenward rolling of the eyes.

And then there is the financial burden. "Well, you do have insurance," people will say—and then end the conversation. Our family has run out of insurance coverage twice. The first five years of my kidney disease alone ran up a tab of a quarter of a million dollars; our part amounted to fifty thousand dollars. My dear husband has had to deal with all of this alone for more than thirty years, most of the time having to work three jobs while taking care of me, our son, and our home.

But please don't imagine I'm complaining; I'm not. I write these words as a challenge to all of us to become more sensitive to what chronic illness does to a family. I am eternally grateful for all those friends and doctors through the years who have poured their lives into my own. Where would I be without the care group that has encouraged and supported me for many years? What would I have done without our good, caring parents, who although a continent away continue to demonstrate their deep concern? How could I have managed without a pastor who has been a great example of what a caring minister should be? (thanks, Bill!) And where would I be without those rare, special friends who have stayed faithful, no matter what?

Through the example and service of these wonderful people, I have been reminded countless times that our Redeemer lives. *He lives!* And as the great sufferer Job said, "After my skin has been destroyed, yet in my flesh I will see God; I myself will see him with my own eyes—I, and not another" (Job 19:26,27).

Ake and Kari continue to reach out to people who desperately need a touch from God. Ake now serves on a pastoral staff of a large church in Portland, Oregon, while Kari (when her health allows) counsels young Christians who find themselves in many kinds of distress. Frequent illnesses and occasional hospitalizations may slow Kari down, but she's determined to continue serving as long as she can. And that looks to be for some time yet. And why not? Her Redeemer lives!

19

A WORK IN PROGRESS

Those misguided folks who believe that the only people stricken with terrifying diseases are sinners and weak, faithless believers would have a hard time explaining Brenda Urda. All of her life, Brenda was a vibrant, faith-filled Christian especially gifted at encouraging people in their personal walks with God. And yet her genuine and growing faith in the Living God did not prevent the suffering she was called upon to endure.

In October of 1988, Brenda Urda was a twenty-eight-year-old Navy wife and registered nurse beaming with pride over the birth of her second son, Travis. One morning she felt a lump in her right breast; thinking it was only a clogged milk duct, she put the problem out of her mind until her six-week postpartum check.

At that time her doctor had the same thought and suggested she wait another six months to see if it would clear up. When nothing changed by the next examination, the doctor sent her to a surgeon "just in case." The surgeon recommended the lump be removed so she "wouldn't have to worry about it anymore" and mentioned that if by some "weird chance" it was something serious, no more time would have been wasted.

Good thing. The fibrous mass discovered below a fluid-filled cyst turned out to be cancer. When she heard the diagnosis, Brenda ran next door to a dear friend and neighbor, fell sobbing into her arms, and shared the horrible news. A few minutes later she called her husband, Ted, to tell him. He came right home from work and the frightened pair headed for their bedroom, laid on the bed, and wept and prayed together. Later that day Brenda gathered her courage to call her folks. "It broke my heart to hear the anguish in my mother's voice," she said. "Several times that night I awoke, hoping that this was all just a bad dream. Morning came and realization started to sink in. I felt like I wanted to vomit."

A few days later her first son Kyle found her crying. "Why are you crying, Mommy?" he asked. She told him she was sad and in his little voice he started singing "God is near," over and over. "Did you learn that in Sunday School?" Brenda asked. "No," came the answer. "Why did you sing that song?" she wondered. "Just because," he said as he toddled off. The encounter gave Brenda great encouragement and hope and she said softly, "God, thank you for speaking to me through the voice of my child."

Brenda decided to have the lymph nodes from under her arm removed and to begin radiation treatments. Five of the twenty-three nodes turned out to be cancerous and a mastectomy was scheduled, to be followed by six months of chemotherapy. Six months after chemo Brenda underwent reconstructive surgery and at last felt as if all the "hurdles" were finally behind her.

"Confronting death gives a new perspective on life," Brenda said. "As the days, months and finally years passed, I thought about cancer less and less. Although I was counseling other women who had been diagnosed with breast cancer, the fear of my cancer recurring lessened as each year passed."

Yet about five years later a series of intense back and neck spasms landed her in the hospital for tests. X-rays came back negative and she started physical therapy, but the spasms soon returned. "One night I woke up and needed to use the bathroom," Brenda said. "I couldn't lift my head up so I put my body over the side of the couch so I could kneel on the floor. Then I propped my elbows on the couch and used my hands to lift my head up. I cried out loud to God to save me and heal me from the unbearable pain, but the room remained silent."

In March of 1995 Brenda's oncologist referred her to orthopedics to see if they could determine the cause of her spasms. A multitude of spinal X-rays revealed the cancer had spread to the bones in her neck. This time "My protective mechanisms took over," Brenda said. "I didn't cry, didn't feel sick, I didn't feel at all. It was as if I was on autopilot."

Her doctor put an X-ray film up on the screen for her to view and instead of seeing white, dense bone, she saw a huge, dark black hole. Brenda kept asking the doctor what else this could possibly be; he named a few things, then told her, "Brenda, it's not something else." The hole was so severe that doctors scheduled an immediate MRI; it revealed the cancer had spread to her skull, sternum, multiple ribs and vertebrae. A large portion of her right pelvis was eaten away and her left thigh bone also had a large hole. The only good news was that the scan showed no cancer in any organs or soft tissue.

Brenda was given a hard plastic collar to wear around her neck twenty-four hours a day as well as a walker to decrease her chances of falling. "If the vertebrae in my neck broke," she said, "the doctors said the result could be catastrophic—death. I felt like a walking time bomb." She dreaded having to call her parents with the catastrophic news. In the previous few years her sister had lost a baby, her grandmother died, and her mother had almost died of complications from a relatively "simple" test.

Orthopedic surgeons wanted to fuse Brenda's skull to her spine—even though she might wake up paralyzed and without a voice—then cement and pin her right pelvis and put a rod down her left thigh bone. She refused. "If the cancer was going to take my life, I would die in one piece," she said. "What was the purpose of going through all that if the cancer would kill me anyway?"

At home one evening her children crawled into bed and asked her, point blank, "Mommy, can this kill you?" Brenda's heart broke as she answered "yes" and saw the look on their faces and heard them gasp. They talked about heaven and discussed how, if she were to die, she would be in heaven with Jesus waiting for them to join her some day. They all cried together and Brenda pleaded, "God, please don't make me do this."

Soon the radiation oncologist decided to radiate Brenda's neck vertebrae, right pelvis, and left thigh bone. Unwanted side effects soon appeared—nausea, diarrhea, tiredness, dry mouth, and extreme sore throat. Brenda lost forty pounds and became so weak she spent her days in a recliner chair.

Yet in time, Brenda's health and strength began to improve and her blood work returned to normal. She wondered if she had been healed—but during the summer of 1996 her back started hurting again. Another MRI showed more destruction of vertebrae; one had almost totally disintegrated. Doctors worried that the collapse of one or more vertebrae would sever Brenda's spinal cord and therefore recommended further radiation.

God, I can't believe I have to do this again! she thought. She kept praying that God would miraculously intervene before she had to endure radiation again—but tears rolled down her cheeks as she heard the slam of the familiar lead door and the machine bombarded her body with radiation once again. After three treatments Brenda decided she had had enough. Her husband and parents opposed her quitting radiation, but she was so sure of God's direction that there was no changing her mind. Her health continued to decline and Brenda admitted "it hurt me to see my husband and parents suffering because of my decision," but no amount of discussion changed minds on either side.

"Throughout our married life I had come to realize that Brenda would latch onto and believe 'what could be' whereas I based my judgment on what 'was,'" Ted said. "We differed widely in our decision-making process and recognized our differences. In my mind, her decision was simply one more example of how we differed in making decisions. On the other hand, I could not deny the extent of her prayer life and that she was at peace with her decision. I could not claim the same prayer relationship with God. I was too busy trying to run the house and keep things as normal as possible for our boys. I understood how Brenda felt, but couldn't fully comprehend it, nor did I agree that it was the right decision. But I was willing to accept it. It was just part of our marriage—agreeing to disagree, harmoniously."

Into this dark situation God still managed to inject great doses of hope and encouragement. One episode in particular touched Brenda's heart. As she told it,

"While listening to our local Christian radio station one day, I heard that a Twila Paris concert was coming to our area in a few months. Twila is my favorite Christian artist. Over the years, the words and music she has written have spoken to my heart and ministered to me in so many ways. I remember praying right then, 'Lord, if there's any way I could go to the concert, and if it's your will, it would really be special for me.' Since I could sit up only by holding myself up with my arms, I thought going to the concert was pretty much an impossibility. Time went by, and the concert was forgotten.

"A few weeks before the concert, a friend mentioned to me that she was thinking about going to the concert. My friend knew how much I loved Twila's music, and to my surprise she offered to call the Christian events center that was holding the concert to see if there would be a way to accommodate me.

"Days later my friend called back to let me know that not only were the details worked out, but the events center graciously offered me a free ticket! All I needed to bring was a folding cot. I could watch the whole concert while lying down in comfort!

"I was so excited about the turn of events and was so grateful to God. What a precious gift God was giving me. After many months of lying in pain on the couch, I had the opportunity to do something 'normal.' The same afternoon I learned of the free ticket, my neighbor called from work to see how I was doing. I asked her if by some chance she had a folding cot, and she said yes! God was providing for *all* my needs for the concert, no matter how small. To me, it was not 'just coincidence' that my neighbor called that afternoon and that she 'just happened' to have a cot; it was God's specific provision.

"The evening of the concert came. My husband, friend and I watched from the balcony. My cot was placed on top of six chairs in order to get me high enough to see over the railing while lying down. What a sight!

"Each song pierced my heart. I felt God speaking to me through the words, encouraging me to persevere in the course he had planned for me. Press on. Run the race.

"Six weeks later, though, I felt as if I were at the end of my rope. I opened my Bible to Psalms. David's word became the cry of my heart. For several hours I wept while reading the Psalms out loud in first person. I told God how bitter this trial was, asked 'how long, Lord?' and poured out my heart before my Father.

"When my children came home from school I tried to pull myself together. The phone rang and my oldest son answered. He put his hand over the receiver and his eyes were wide with excitement. 'Mom, it's Twila Paris!' *Oh, great,* I thought, *one of my friends is a comedian.*

"I took the phone and said hello. To my surprise, a voice on the other end said, 'Brenda, this is Twila Paris.' I just about fell off the couch! Twila told me how Dave Dravecky had contacted her and told her about the lengths to which I had gone in order to see her concert. He asked Twila if she would give me an encouragement call. Twila was so kind and gracious; I didn't feel like 'a star' had reached down to pat my head, but that a sister in the Lord was acting as a servant, washing my feet with her words.

"After hanging up the phone, I was overwhelmed with a sense of God's love, care, and presence. He knew right where I was that afternoon, emotionally and physically. He hadn't forgotten or abandoned me, but sent Twila's phone call just when I needed it. It was such a powerful reminder of his faithfulness."

And yet Brenda's struggles continued. In January 1997 her sixty-three-year-old father died suddenly. By February she herself lay in bed twenty-four hours a day. "Every movement required a great deal of effort," she said. "The days were long and I felt so lonely and isolated, but God continued to pour out his strength and grace. Even though suffering is so painful and I would never choose it, I'm thankful that God loves me too much to leave me the way I was. The refiner's fire is purifying the garbage out of my life. My heart's desire is to be a woman of godly character—I only wish there were an easier way for me to develop it!"

Ted assumed all housekeeping responsibilities—cooking, cleaning, laundry, and chauffeuring the boys to their activities. Women at the Urdas' church also helped by providing meals and cleaning the house every other week.

In the ensuing months Brenda's pain diminished and her strength gradually increased. She still had to use support when sitting and walking, but she called herself "a work in progress" and added, "God has promised never to leave or forsake me. This is not a journey I would have chosen, but I wouldn't trade it for anything. The growth process has been painful, but my relationship with the Lord has grown dramatically."

By October 1997, the pain in Brenda's spine had become so great that she was no longer able to negotiate the stairs, and so remained in her upstairs bedroom. By Thanksgiving she had become confused and a hospice nurse advised Ted that this usually meant the cancer had spread to the liver. Just a few days later, on December 4, Brenda died.

"Despite her condition and prognosis," Ted said, "Brenda never gave up hope of being healed. Her compassionate spirit and enduring faith were an inspiration to all who knew her. In the last year of her life, Brenda became totally reliant on God for her survival. Whether she lived or died, Brenda placed her trust in the only true hope she had: God."

20

A HARD ROAD BACK

This is a story of courage starring two remarkable people, a mother and daughter team who together are tenaciously battling a whirlwind of suffering. Their story is long and its ending already seems written—yet every time I hear it I am encouraged more strongly to "keep on keeping on." I hope you will be, too.

Proverbs 13:12 speaks a world of truth to Jenny Unger: "Hope deferred makes the heart sick, but a longing fulfilled is a tree of life."

"We all learn pretty quick in life that we don't always get what we want, and things don't always turn out the way we plan," she says. "But sometimes God takes us by the hand and leads us to a place where our hope and faith is tested—and for a time it seems as if we don't get anything we want and nothing turns out the way we plan. We face disappointment after disappointment and loss after loss until we become so beat up and confused in our grief that we don't know which way is up." Jenny's main source of discouragement has always centered around the trials of her daughter, Chatra.

Chatra was born healthy and beautiful in August 1982, a joyous gift from God after Jenny had suffered four miscarriages in the previous five years. The next two and a half years were filled with awe and gratitude for a new baby girl. Every smile and new trick, Chatra's first words and first steps, were all miracles to Jenny. She cherished her daughter and every day prayed for her health and well-being.

But on Father's Day 1984, before Chatra had turned three years old, she was diagnosed with leukemia. Jenny immediately responded to God with blazing anger. She looked up to heaven and screamed, "Why this and why now? I don't get it! You've already taken four babies from me, and then you give me a beautiful, healthy little girl for two short years—and now you ask me to watch her die a slow and painful death of cancer? What a horrible, cruel joke!" Yet despite her anger and confusion, in her heart she knew her only hope and comfort lay in God.

Jenny and Rick Unger were quickly assured by the oncologist that childhood leukemia no longer meant a death sentence; the cure rate for their daughter's malady was then reckoned at about eighty percent. Chatra stood a great chance of recovering full health.

Chatra survived endless days in hospitals, hundreds of injections and spinal taps, blood and platelet transfusions, a suppressed immune system and long periods of isolation, sleeplessness and bouts of five to six hours of uninterrupted vomiting caused by the toxicity of the chemo drugs. The ordeal lasted for two long years, but Jenny had complete hope and faith that her daughter would be healed and the cancer eradicated.

For a year after chemo, Chatra reported to the doctor for monthly check-ups and blood work. Her health steadily improved for ten months; but once more on Father's Day, Chatra's cancer returned and Jenny's anger at God slid into massive disappointment. "I was so disheartened," she said. "I just couldn't believe that the God I loved and trusted so much would allow this kind of pain in my life again. Somehow I believed that if I did all the right things, prayed all the right prayers and surrendered my will to the best of my ability, that I was earning a right to God's favor. If I was a good little girl, then my heavenly Father would certainly protect me and my family from all evil."

Stunned that God would allow Chatra's suffering to continue, Jenny came to agree with a statement C. S. Lewis made when his own wife was stricken with cancer: "It is not that I am in much danger of ceasing to believe in God. The real danger is coming to believe such dreadful things about him. The conclusion I dread is not, So there is no God after all, but, So this is what God is really like."

Doctors encouraged the Ungers not to give up hope and explained they hadn't treated the cancer aggressively enough. This time they would pull out all the stops and give Chatra the most aggressive chemo protocol available, plus radiation therapy. They warned it would be difficult, but with the new plan, doctors were convinced they would beat the cancer.

This time around, however, the ordeal was far worse. It's no big deal to lose your hair when you're three, but it's a whole different challenge when you're six and going to school every day and all your friends are wearing pigtails and pretty barrettes in their hair. Everywhere Chatra went, adults would stare and children would poke fun. She missed almost a whole year of school, most of it spent in isolation. Chatra couldn't comprehend why she couldn't join her friends. For the first time she also realized she was different, that something was "wrong" with her. Thoughtless people recounted stories of all those they knew who had died of cancer; several of Chatra's hospital friends had died of cancer; and she became increasingly fearful of her own death. She began talking a lot about death and suffered recurring nightmares. She kept asking her mother what it would feel like to be dead.

Once at school during recess Chatra held her own mock funeral. She lay in the bottom of a play boat on the playground and had the other children bring pretend flowers and cry over her. The game was discovered when some of the children began having nightmares and their parents called the school. The game was discontinued, but for weeks afterward Chatra continued to lie alone every day at recess in the bottom of her boat. She was not only in extreme physical pain, but also in great emotional pain. And it needed to be expressed.

"Grief demands expression and there is no escape," Jenny says. "It grabs you in its massive jaws and seems to tear you into little pieces. Now, you may think that because God had consistently proved himself faithful to us in the past, that when these new challenges came along in our lives, it would be easy to relax. Not so. In our frail humanity, each new heartache is like no other heartache that has gone before and our emotional pain suddenly overrides our knowledge of God's purpose in our lives. The natural grieving process diminishes our sense of hope and we become numb to anything except our pain."

Chatra began radiation therapy. Radiation is the only treatment without immediate physical pain, but it caused the deepest emotional scars for Jenny. "After they made three permanent tattoos on her head, they fashioned a plastic mask of her little face," she explained. "For each treatment they laid her on her back on a hard, metal table, strapped her down, and placed the mask over her face in order to bolt her head immovably to the table. As she lay there, helpless and frightened, I could only watch through a window in a separate room. For the first time since her birth, I was unable to offer her any comfort or encouragement. We were physically and emotionally cut off from one another. The treatments were short, but I thought I would die from the heartache. I couldn't stop saying to myself, 'What in the world are you doing, Jenny? You are giving these people permission to fry your daughter's brain!'"

Of course, while the procedure sounds like some form of medieval torture, it is absolutely necessary. Any body movement would reduce the chances of targeting the exact locations of tumors. Such immobilizing techniques are vital to successful treatment.

Doctors warned that the treatments would take away ten percent of Chatra's intelligence and unpredictable amounts of her cognitive thinking. They were correct. The older Chatra gets, the more difficulties she has in school. Facts that used to be so easy for her to grasp are now a struggle to retain. Sometimes she comes home upset from school and says, "Mom, I feel so stupid. Today I couldn't remember how to subtract. I just stared at my paper and couldn't remember anything. I was embarrassed to ask for help and it felt like I was learning it for the very first time. What's wrong with me?"

For nearly three weeks during the radiation treatments, Chatra slept up to twenty hours a day. She lost a lot of weight but somehow struggled through another two years of trauma. The family waited apprehensively through the next year, worrying about another relapse. But when her ten-month relapse anniversary came and went and the eleventh month passed with no sign of cancer, doctors said, "You guys are on your way now. We want to see you only every three months for the next year. We don't expect any more relapses."

Less than two weeks later, Chatra's symptoms returned and she was diagnosed for the third time with cancer. Now Chatra immediately began begging her mother to let her die. "Mom," she said, "I really can't do this again, and besides, I'm not afraid to die anymore. Jesus told me that it would be OK and when I'm in heaven I won't hurt anymore." Jenny broke down and cried in her daughter's lap. "Don't cry, Mommy," Chatra said. "It'll be OK. I'll miss you and Daddy in heaven, but it will seem like only a minute before you will be with me again. Plus, my first puppy Angel will be there and all my friends who died of cancer will be there, too."

Yet despite Chatra's protests, chemo began again. Every time the Ungers would head for the clinic, Chatra became hysterical. She'd cry and beg not to be taken. "I'd rather die," she screamed. "You can't make me cooperate!" She directed her grief and anger at her mother, and as her pain increased, so did Jenny's.

At that point the family scheduled a conference with specialists at Stanford Medical University. They declared a bone marrow transplant was not an option for Chatra because the intensity of her previous treatments made it unlikely she could survive the procedure. To Jenny it was the end of the road and she left Stanford absolutely hopeless. Overcome with a sense of doom, she "went over the edge" and lost perspective, lost sight of God's mercy, and lost all hope. She couldn't hug or even read to her daughter without thinking that it might be the last time. Jenny had come to accept that Chatra would die, so she couldn't understand why God would allow her continued suffering. Paradoxically, she became increasingly angry that Chatra was still alive: "Now, go figure that one out, will you!" she says today.

Meanwhile, her marriage began to weaken under the constant pressures. She and Rick were forced into bankruptcy from mounting medical bills and their vehicle was repossessed. Jenny gave up any personal ministry at church and basically gave up on God. "In my mind, God had put me on the shelf and abandoned me," she explained. "I felt I no longer had any useful purpose. For the first time in my life, I could find no comfort in God's Word. I literally felt like my flesh was melting from my bones and I would gradually just cease to exist. I ceased asking God for anything. I figured, *why put forth the effort to hope for anything good when I'm always gravely disappointed and only bad things happen anyway?* I stopped praying. I stopped going to church and I stopped reading my Bible. It got to the point where I couldn't even speak God's name; it was too painful. All hope was deferred for me and my heart was now very, very sick."

Yet once Jenny decided to resist God's presence in her life, there was nowhere to go except down. As the weeks passed, she became more and more paralyzed by her shame and emptiness. She didn't know how to make things right again and her longing for reconciliation increased; the deepest part of her soul cried out for God to rescue her.

In her darkest hour, God broke through to her in a little book titled, *When sorely afflicted or in pain or struck by unreasonable tragedy . . . MAY I HATE GOD?* The words of the book completely disarmed her and enticed her back into communion with her Lord. Through some wonderful illustrations, Jenny was able to embrace the life-changing truth that it didn't matter what she brought before God; it mattered only that she came. If all she had was pain and confusion, he would gladly accept it. God gave her hope once more and very tenderly provided a way for her back to his throne.

"He showed me that no matter how far out there I get, or how blinded I become because of my pain, in his time, he will always lead me back," Jenny said. "That is what his grace is all about! In spite of me, he has promised to complete in me the work that he started so many years ago when I first asked him into my life. In spite of life's circumstances, disappointments, losses and heartache, God is faithful. He is true and he is all-powerful. He can be trusted! God restored my hope and fulfilled the longing in my soul."

And note this: Jenny says such a thing even though she is still part of a family in chronic grief whose finances are still "dreadful" and whose daughter is still fighting a losing battle with cancer. Recently Chatra suffered yet another relapse and will continue for the rest of her life on the doses of chemotherapy that her body can tolerate. Pain management and quality of life are the family's new goals.

Jenny wants everyone to know that Chatra is the real hero of this story. "Chatra is the one who is awesome," she declares. "Rick and I both proudly proclaim her as our own personal hero. We have yet to meet anyone with more tenacious courage or determination. We count it our greatest privilege in life to be her parents. It is a powerful thing to watch God carve his likeness into someone so young. She is an inspiration to everyone she meets. It doesn't take long to recognize that she lives every day of her life with an incredible passion and determination to fulfill her goals and dreams with whatever time God may choose to bless her with."

Jenny knows that when Chatra's days are over and her daughter goes to be with the Lord, she will face her own greatest challenge. "But in the meantime, my family is united and strong," she says. "Because of our experience, we all love a little deeper, laugh a little louder, hug each other more often, and embrace the simple pleasures of this life. Today I can stand in the confidence of God's faithful grace and mercy and know that he will prevail in my life. His will will be completed. And no matter what path I walk in this life, I rest assured that I will walk the next with my God."

One scripture verse in particular, Psalm 57:1 (LIVING BIBLE), strengthens her confidence. It is a text Jenny has grown to love:

O God, have pity, for I am trusting you! I will hide beneath the shadow of your wings until this storm is past.

PART THREE

THE STRENGTH TO DIE

21

A GRAND SLAM OVER
HEAVEN'S CENTER FIELD WALL

On September 29, 1995, the Outreach of Hope received word that a twenty-three-year-old baseball player named Chris Priest had been diagnosed with testicular cancer. Already he had undergone surgery and was receiving chemotherapy. I was out of the office at the time but planned to call Chris when I returned. Over the next two and a half years our staff did what we could to encourage the Priests through their terrible ordeal. Chris and I talked baseball. Throughout his battle against cancer, Chris made it his goal to strengthen and encourage others. It's a commitment he never abandoned.

Chris Priest grew up with a baseball mitt in one hand and a bat in the other. He almost had no choice; his two older brothers coaxed him into shagging balls for them when he was still a toddler. Baseball was as much a part of Chris's life as learning his ABCs and figuring out how to tie his shoes. His brothers taught him everything they knew about the game and his skills blossomed by constantly playing with older boys.

But it also took work. Many times Chris came home from batting practice, hands bleeding from long hours of swinging and making hard contact. He played summer ball in the wooden bat leagues to prepare himself for a career in the majors and while his friends held down full-time jobs to make money for cars and dates, Chris worked odd jobs wherever they fit around his baseball schedule. He had a dream, and he was committed to turning it into reality.

At age fourteen Chris played in the Little League World Series in San Juan, Puerto Rico, and won the U. S. batting title.

He made the Plainfield varsity team all four years of high school, where he received "All Conference" honors each year and was named Most Valuable Player of the Little Seven Conference his senior year in 1990. He attended Lewis University on a baseball scholarship (where he batted .451) and three times was selected as an all-American. It surprised him when no professional team drafted him out of college, but Chris attacked his disappointment by playing in 1994 for the Lethbridge Mounties of the Pioneer League in Canada. Major leaguer Andre Dawson had played there years before, and Chris decided he would try to break Dawson's home run mark. He did. Major league scouts noticed and picked him up in 1995.

When his mom returned home from work one day Chris said, "Mama, you know what you're looking at?"

She knew by his enormous smile something was up, but couldn't guess what. "Sure," she said, "I'm looking at my boy."

"No!" Chris replied, "You're looking at a *Minnesota Twin!*" That year *Baseball America* called Chris "the player to watch in the upcoming season."

After spring training in Florida, Chris joined the Twins' Class A affiliate in Visalia, California. In the middle of a blistering hitting streak he noticed a sharp twinge in his back; his trainer told him he'd pulled a muscle and ordered physical therapy. The pain grew worse; the trainer added whirlpool treatments. But still the pain increased. Soon the team placed Chris on the disabled list, then sent him home to his family doctor. Nobody expected what came next. "I have some bad news for you," the doctor said. "I think Chris has cancer."

Cancer! Chris sat motionless on the examining table, staring at nothing. His promising career, a cherished lifetime dream— gone? How could this be?

In the next few days further tests showed the cancer had spread into his lungs and liver and across his abdomen. Doctors immediately began massive chemotherapy treatments. Serious bleeding followed, requiring an emergency flight to Indianapolis, Indiana, where Chris underwent a series of operations necessary to save his life. His fiancée couldn't take the strain and broke off their engagement. It was the middle of 1995 and Chris was all of twenty-three.

The crisis called for courage—and determination. Chris refused to give up on life, though doctors held out little hope for his survival.

"Not once did I ever hear Chris complain," marveled his mother, Donna. "He looked to Jesus for the strength to help him make it through."

Chris also looked to help others. On his good days, he gave motivational talks at area schools, youth groups, and churches, where he spoke about God and getting life's priorities in order. He volunteered his time to coach promising young ballplayers.

"Mama," he said to Donna one day, "You know what my greatest moment so far in baseball has been?" She didn't know. "It's to see one of my players make a play they didn't know how to make until I taught them. That just makes me feel great!"

Chris often encouraged and comforted the distraught and fearful people he encountered in the hospital. When he was finally allowed to walk the hallways after one major treatment, he heard a woman sobbing convulsively in a waiting room; her husband had just been diagnosed with acute leukemia. Chris slowly approached her, sat down, helped soothe her fears, then prayed with her. Another time he spoke with a fourteen-year-old boy who had attempted suicide; Chris gently told him life is a precious gift. When the mother of Chris's best friend entered the Intensive Care Unit, he repeatedly visited her and arranged for his friend to live with his own family for two months during her slow recuperation.

"Chris always believed in giving something back," said Donna. "That's why he talked to people who were struggling—people with illnesses, drug dealers, people who had suffered loss.

Anybody. He talked about how his priorities were out of whack when he was younger, and how things were different now."[1]

Meanwhile, Chris's body continued to deteriorate. His cancer grew worse and eventually doctors told the family there could be no hope for his recovery.

"Well, it's the ninth inning, there's two outs," Chris said. "Jesus, you're up to bat. There's no other person I would want standing in the batter's box than you. If God sees fit to give me a miracle, I win. If in his sovereign will he takes me home to heaven, I win."

But the game was not yet over and Chris refused to live as a dead man. In June 1997, under the crossed bats of the Will County Cheetah's baseball team, he married new fiancée Melissa Carter at Lewis University's Brennan Field.

Four months later, Melissa became a widow. "The four months we had together felt like a lifetime," she said. "He was like a gift to me. Chris was definitely one-of-a-kind."[2]

At the time of his death, Chris's mother told a newspaper reporter, "It's a great loss. I learned so much from him in the past two and a half years. I thought I knew what love was. I didn't. He showed me."[3]

Chris's body gave up on October 4, 1997—in the words of his mother, "at 10:25 A.M. Chris hit a grand slam over heaven's center field wall and made it safely home." But Chris never gave up. He lived to the full until the very last time his lungs filled with air. At his home-going service, it was said that when Chris became ill, he traded one piece of wood for another—the bat for the cross.

By age twenty-five, Chris knew more about the courage to die than most of us discover in a lifespan three times that long. He's with his Heavenly Father now, but his example of courage lives on. Like him, it can never really die.

Notes

1. Gary Seymour, "Infielder kept winning," *Herald-News*, Joliet, Illinois, Vol. 122, No. 279, page A5.
2. Ibid.
3. Seymour, A1.

22

SURRENDERING EVERYTHING...
BUT HOPE

In late 1995 we received a letter from a man in Carmel, Indiana, who needed to brag about his pastor. The letter writer raved about the weekly church service and said the pastor always had time to do the Lord's work. Doesn't seem especially noteworthy, does it? No doubt your own pastor has a wonderful ministry and always takes time to do the Lord's work, too. But does your pastor suffer from Lou Gehrig's Disease, more properly called Amyotrophic Lateral Sclerosis? The Rev. Tommy Paino does.

ALS is a disease of middle life, affecting primarily men. Its cause is unknown but it always follows the same course: gradual weakening and atrophy of the voluntary muscles, ending in death. There is no known cure. By the time Tommy Paino was asked to contribute to this book in late 1997, his disease had progressed to its later stages. Barring a miracle, Tommy will soon be called home to his Lord. And yet he faces the end with courage and faith.

Something troubled pastor Tommy Paino the day he helped his church move into its new facilities. Boxes and equipment and file cabinets that he once moved with ease had somehow become heavier, bulkier, especially for his right arm and hand. He'd ignored the growing weakness until then, but this move convinced him he shouldn't wait to see a doctor. He suspected the problem was nothing more than carpal tunnel syndrome, but many tests performed over several months revealed a very different diagnosis.

On October 1, 1995, Tommy stood in a spartan office furnished only with two metal chairs and one gleaming examination table. The neurologist walked into the room, told Tommy to sit down, and announced coldly, "Tommy, I'm ninety-nine percent sure that what you have is Lou Gehrig's Disease." Not pausing to let the news sink in, she continued, "That means you can expect to live three to four years. And here's the way this will progress." She then explained how all his voluntary muscles would waste away, leading to total paralysis. Eventually he would die of asphyxiation. Tommy walked out of the office in deep shock.

For one year this faithful pastor struggled with denial and depression. He threw himself into fighting and beating this disease, yet as the months wore on he saw parts of his body shut down. From one day to the next he never knew what part of his body would begin to quit working. His hands were the first to be affected. One day he could click open a pen; the next day, his thumb lacked the strength. Increasing weakness in his hands and arms soon made it difficult to hold a Bible, shake church members' hands, or even type sermons, tasks he had performed as pastor for sixteen years.

The weakness eventually progressed to Tommy's legs, making it more and more difficult to walk. As a devoted runner, he had participated in a mini-marathon every May for the previous seventeen years; May of 1996 marked his last race.

Tommy began having trouble speaking because of the relentless weakening in his throat, tongue, and facial muscles. The disease also affected his chest, limiting his ability to expand and contract his diaphragm to speak. That is particularly troubling for a pastor who depends on his voice to deliver sermons and to speak words of comfort and wisdom to his flock. And even beyond this, fatigue became Tommy's unwelcome but constant companion.

Eventually Tommy came to believe that the Lord was using his disease as a test. God had opened a door to prove the very faith he had preached for twenty-five years. He felt God saying to him, "Now I will test and purify your faith."

"I had always been the type of person who needed to be in control," Tommy says. "For fifteen years I had delivered all the Sunday morning sermons, performed all the weddings and funerals, and counseled anyone who requested it. If there were ever an open house, graduation, or anything else going on, I was there. I would spend up to seventy hours a week working at the church, trying to do it all. After my diagnosis of Lou Gehrig's Disease, I carried that same need to control everything into fighting the disease, tooth and nail. I had an almost compulsive need to keep everything on track.

"But there finally came a time, after one year of dealing with depression, denial, and fighting for control over this disease, that I came to a fork in the road. God asked me, 'Tommy, what are you willing to turn loose and put into my hands? Will you trust me?' In my faith journey, God was asking me to travel new paths of trust."

Part of that journey would take Tommy to a Trappist monastery in Missouri, where he spent three weeks in November alone with God. It became a Gethsemane experience for him in which he relinquished his will to that of the Father. And it was anything but easy.

"I was not a happy camper," Tommy says simply. "It felt very much to me as if I were dying. It's very painful to give up everything. When God asks us to relinquish something, it's as if we ourselves are marching to the cross."

It takes courage to surrender everything, and although Tommy describes himself as someone who is "very wimpy" by nature, he discovered that even the "wimpiest" among us has been given a measure of courage. When the time is right and when we have a chance to use it, it's there at our disposal. By God's grace and with his help, we can all act with courage. He calls this the decision to "let go without giving up."

But what if someone were to say to Tommy, "Sure, it's easy for you to surrender those things in your life. You don't have a choice." How would he respond?

"Oh, but there is a choice," he insists. "The choice is the attitude with which I approach all this. It is possible to accept what is happening to me and yet be resentful and bitter. To surrender to God and be at peace with myself and others, I must get beyond mere acceptance and relinquish everything to God—everything, that is, but hope."

Even after his "surrender retreat" with the Trappist monks, however, Tommy found he still needed to continually relinquish his life, his family, and his church. His prayers today are focused on that difficult task and he finds that he has to retrace old steps repeatedly.

"In that process," he says, "there come a few shining moments where I'm certain that I have actually relinquished my life into God's will. In that moment of total surrender, I am free to pray for resurrection in its proper way. For me, resurrection means healing."

Tommy's wife, Sandy, says "each new day is a new adventure and we wait for God to unfold it before us." In early 1996 Tommy suffered a heart attack and nearly two years later he still clings tenaciously to life. Yet he is ready to go home whenever God calls him, and in the meanwhile he works at continuing to relinquish his life and everything in it to the Lord of the universe. And how does he see the future?

When we last spoke, his body was almost totally paralyzed. He was in a wheelchair, totally dependent on others to provide for his every physical need. He is learning that nothing compares to knowing God. "The things that are bound by time are but a blip on the screen of life," he says. "I have been given this sliver of time to set my heart on those things that are of God and those things that are eternal." That's how he continues to live without losing faith for today or hope for tomorrow.

23

A WIN-WIN SITUATION

Wisdom, strength, and courage aren't the exclusive property of grizzled veterans of life who count their birthdays in scores of years. Sometimes those qualities rise to prominence in boys and girls still in their early teens. Adam Gustafson is one such young man of extraordinary courage and faith.

We first learned of Adam's case a few months after he was diagnosed with inoperable brain cancer. His family lives near the ministry in Colorado Springs and so we took a special interest in his valiant battle. From the beginning I was struck by Adam's positive outlook and his unwillingness to dwell on the negative. He inspired me to live whatever length of life I have for the glory of God. His example still amazes me.

"I'm in a win-win situation. If God heals me I can ride my bike and I win. If God doesn't heal me, I go to heaven to be with him, and I still win."

No father wants to hear such words from his teenage son, but that's exactly what Adam Gustafson told his dad just months before his death from inoperable brain cancer. It's strange how the same words can fill a man's heart with both wonder and dread, blessing and fear—and yet those were precisely the conflicting emotions that flooded Jon's soul.

Adam's life was never easy. "He had a difficult time from the beginning," Jon says. "When he was still in the womb, at about three months, his mother spent a week in the hospital with dehydration. Barb suffered from nausea throughout the pregnancy. Maybe Adam was in a hurry to get on with his life, because we had just gotten settled into the labor room when the nurse informed us that we should be on our way to the delivery room. Ten minutes later, Adam was in my arms."

When Adam was two years old he began displaying some personality traits that would serve him well later on. He was a persistent kid, although at the time his dad thought the word "stubborn" fit better. Jon would put his son to bed, get him to say his prayers, and turn out the lights. Barb and Jon would then get settled in the family room when they'd see "a cute little face" peek around the corner. Jon took Adam back to bed, kissed him, told him to stay in bed, and warned him that if he got up again he would be spanked. No sooner had Jon sat down again than he'd look up to see the same little face peeking around the corner once more. Now Jon faced a dilemma: how could he laugh and give discipline at the same time? He had to suppress his grin and do what he had threatened to do— four or five times every night! It took Adam four months to realize this was a battle he couldn't win.

School was not easy for Adam, primarily because he suffered from Attention Deficit Disorder, a neurological condition that makes it difficult to translate knowledge in the brain to the written or spoken word. It often took Adam four or five times longer to "get" an answer than it took his classmates, and that naturally led to great frustration and frequent teasing.

Because Adam knew what it was like to be ridiculed, he wanted to make sure that anyone in a position to be taunted would know they had at least one friend. One boy told Adam's parents that after he transferred to Adam's class, Adam was the first person to talk to him and tell him that he would be his friend. There was also the neighborhood kid whose friendship no one wanted—except Adam. When Jon asked his son about it, Adam simply replied, "He's not so bad. Besides, he needed a friend."

Adam's persistence, patience, and kind heart would serve him well as he began his thirteenth year. The first sign of the coming battle appeared at basketball practice. When he started having trouble catching the ball and running the floor without falling, his coach became concerned for his safety. About the same time Adam began suffering bouts of dizziness and lack of coordination. His parents thought the problems resulted from his ADD medication, but taking him off the medicine didn't seem to help.

Then on January 15, 1994, Adam took the family's Rottweiler for a walk. When the dog bolted, Adam fell and scraped his face; that night he had trouble walking up the stairs. The next day Barb took him in to be examined and the doctor suggested they see if his condition improved over the weekend. When it didn't, Adam went in for a CT scan. That's when the Gustafsons learned their son didn't have a concussion as feared, but some kind of growth on his brain stem. That night doctors took a picture of his brain using an MRI, and the next morning at 8:00 A.M. the neurologist gravely told Jon and Barb that their son had a brain tumor. "Your son has no more than eighteen months to live," he said. The date was January 18, 1994, "the worst day of my life," in Jon's words. "Cancer is a four letter word that happens to have six letters," he says today.

When Jon and Barb told their son the news, he began crying. "Daddy, I don't want to die," he sobbed.

The tears didn't last long, however. Throughout his ordeal Adam chose to believe that God would heal him; his conviction never wavered. He saw kids his own age in his treatment room die from the same disease he had—but he would turn to his mom and steadfastly say, "I'm really sorry that happened, but that is not going to happen to me. I'm not going to die." Eventually Adam named his tumor "Fred" and started repeating the phrase, "Drop dead, Fred."

Only after his death did his parents learn that Adam had asked a few friends to "look after" his mom if he didn't survive. Such an attitude typified Adam: He was more concerned about how his condition might affect his mom than how it affected him.

When word of Adam's plight got out, hundreds of cards and letters began pouring in. Adam always wanted to be a police officer like his dad, and the Chief of the Colorado Springs Police

Department made Adam an honorary police officer with his own official ID card. The Colorado Springs Tactical Enforcement Unit gave Adam his own call sign (his radio moniker) and a hat with his name and call sign on it. The Teller County Sheriff made him an honorary Deputy Sheriff with his own badge; he was even sworn in on TV. John Elway, Adam's favorite NFL football player, signed a football for him, while two offensive linemen for Elway's Denver Broncos came to Adam's fourteenth birthday party, bringing a football autographed by the team. Other autographed items also arrived: a football signed by the Colorado State University Rams; baseballs from Jason Bates and me; a cap from Dante Bichette of the Colorado Rockies. Adam couldn't understand why all these people would do such nice things for him. He was the same person he'd always been, after all. So why the fuss?

Adam's growing tumor eventually paralyzed part of his left side. One day he sat with his mom in his room upstairs when Barb looked out the window to see neighborhood kids playing in the empty lot across the street. She broke down and through hot tears told Adam, "You should be out there playing with them!"

"Don't cry, Mom," Adam replied, "I'm doing fine."

Adam learned to enjoy what he could do and refused to dwell on what he couldn't do. Adam's best friend later said he never heard Adam say anything like, "This really stinks." He stubbornly chose to dwell on the positive.

Adam made between one hundred fifty and two hundred trips to the doctor for treatments and checkups and the family sought alternative treatments for him in Houston. On one trip something went wrong and Adam told his nurse that he hurt. She sprang into action because she knew Adam never complained. "We knew that if he said it hurt, there was something seriously wrong," she said. She was right; Adam's tumor had begun to bleed, resulting in the complete paralysis of his left side.

Adam spent a year and half in a wheelchair and had to depend on others for basic functions such as going to the bathroom, taking a bath, or getting dressed. Yet he never complained, never talked about his humiliation. The only thing Jon ever heard from his son was, "Thanks, Dad, I don't know how I'd make it without you. I love you!"

Adam loved to play games and became good at almost any card game you can name. One friend who visited Adam overnight later told his mom he wasn't going to complain when things didn't go right for him because, "Here is Adam, he can't get up and walk, and he has to put his cards in a tray because he can't use his left hand. Yet he is smiling and laughing and having a great time."

*A*dam's *earthly laughter was quelled on November 4, 1995, when he died. "I thank God every day for giving me the privilege of being the dad of Adam Gustafson—a fifteen-year-old young man who exemplifies courage, faith, care, and love for those around him," his dad said. In a letter to the Outreach of Hope, Jon wrote, "Heaven is a place all Christians look forward to seeing, but because we have just recently walked to heaven's door and put our son's hand in the Lord's hand, it has taken on a whole new meaning. Yes, Adam won and even though we miss him more than we can say, we know that someday just as we showed him the beauty of God's creation on earth, Adam will show us the place God has prepared for us."*

24

LIKE CREAM CHEESE TO
A KOSHER BAGEL

Sometimes a death sentence is the best tool God has for giving new life to a perishing man. It was that way, at least, for David Gordon when doctors told him he had Stage 4 adenocarcinoma and could expect to live no more than a few months.

If anyone had told me at the beginning of 1996 that I would accept Christ as my personal Lord and Savior, I would have bet all the money I ever made against it. It isn't that I disliked Christ or was against him in any way; it's just that I'm Jewish. My mother is Jewish, my father is Jewish, all of my uncles, aunts, and everyone in my ancestry is Jewish. In fact, you can trace my Jewish roots all the way to Abraham.

So why would I come to Christ? To me, Christ was someone to whom condemned prisoners and lost souls cling in their most terrible time of need. But I had always lived a good life and conducted myself in a highly moral and ethical manner, not only in my business, but also as a father and with all my fellow human beings. And I had done it all by myself, with no help from God.

But on December 6, 1996, I was diagnosed with adenocarcinoma, a cancer which has spread to my liver, lungs, pancreas and bones. My doctors gave me six months to live, told me surgery was not an option, and that chemotherapy might not be effective. Worse yet, I was told I would probably be confined to a wheelchair because of the massive tumors in my lower spine and right hip.

When we're faced with frightening words like these, the most horrible things enter our mind. First comes panic, then a deeprooted fear. Whether we choose to fight the cancer or accept imminent death, we face an incredible journey, both emotionally and physically.

It also takes a devastating toll on our family members. They feel helpless. At least the one with cancer can do something to fight it; but loved ones have no idea what to do. Anyone who has ever faced cancer will tell you courage is the one thing you need most of all—and yet at the time it seems totally out of reach, unattainable. You feel lost, with no way out.

That's exactly how I felt December 6, 1996. I had no idea that within two weeks my sister, Rosanne, would help me find a path of rescue.

R osanne had fought her own difficult battles. In her first week of life she caught a staph infection and lost a lung. At age two she was burned when her crib caught fire. At age thirteen she was raped and doctors told her she would never have children. A few years later she began a long bout with alcoholism, then suffered through a terrible marriage filled with verbal and emotional abuse. In 1991 she learned she had contracted hepatitis C. Finally, she was diagnosed with a rare form of skin cancer. But seven years ago she found her way to Christ and gained all the strength, peace, and will to survive that any human being could need. Today she is married and has given birth (contrary to the doctors) to two precious boys.

When Rosanne heard about my cancer, she advised me the time had come to look to the New Testament for inner peace and solace. She passionately tried to convince me Christ was the only way to escape my predicament. That was hard for me to stomach. In my entire life I never asked anything from God. Anyway, it seemed futile for me to try and connect with Jesus. I could envision God saying to me, "Oh, so *now* you want to come to me? You're faced with cancer and could possibly die soon, so you want me to help you? You didn't need me before, but now all of a sudden, you wanna do business? I don't think so. The answer is **NO!!**"

As a young boy I occasionally went to church with friends for weddings, confirmations, and the like. I remember seeing a large cross with a statuette of Jesus hanging on it. This really scared me, because as a Jew, I figured I was partly responsible for putting him there. So how could I turn to him as an adult?

I was scared and without a trace of hope. In the two weeks following my diagnosis, I checked out a ton of books to understand the cancer. What I discovered didn't encourage me; for the first time in my life, I contemplated suicide. I began to think of the pain my children would have to endure, as well as my own physical agony. Would I be reduced to something like a survivor of a Nazi concentration camp? Would I lie helpless in life support, with tubes and IV lines sprouting out of me like some medical pin cushion? I couldn't bear the thought—yet after a period of calm, I realized I could never take my own life.

Instead, I did what my sister suggested. I opened the New Testament and began to explore the Scriptures. Many passages spoke powerfully to me, but what stood out most were the promises God seemed to be making. The more I read, the more I saw what God wanted to do for me. He was telling me I would be OK no matter what! And all God wanted from me was my faith and a genuine relationship with himself.

I discovered that the eleventh chapter of Hebrews starts out by asking, "What is faith?" then in the second verse answers its own question: "Faith is the confident assurance that what we hope for will happen." At last I understood clearly what that passage means. It isn't the end result that matters, as much as the faith we display in our walk with Christ. That is where peace comes from, not in seeing some particular end result. The firm belief that I am not alone carries me from day to day with all the strength I need.

I phoned my sister and told her that I had decided to accept Jesus for what he is: God's true gift to the Jews, the Messiah. I was now ready to accept Jesus as my personal Lord and Savior. My sister immediately booked herself on the next flight from Orange County to Monterey, California. She wasn't taking any chances; she had a hot prospect and had to close the deal before he changed his mind! And so on December 16, 1996, the two of us found ourselves down on our knees in my living room and I asked Christ into my heart forever. From that moment, I no longer feared the cross. Today I cling to it like cream cheese to a kosher bagel.

The greatest thing I learned as a baby Christian is that God doesn't think like we do. God is so filled with unconditional love for us that he'll take us any way he can get us—any time, any place—right up to the moment of our death. What a beautiful truth about a perfect love!

Because I now bask in that perfect love, I can take whatever life throws at me. In the past twelve weeks I have been involved in a trial medical experiment at Stanford University. The trial was supposed to shrink my tumors enough to give me more time to try other chemotherapy agents and thus prolong my life. Last week I was told I was being released from the program because it was not working; the tumors in my liver had actually grown. In the past I would have cracked open my collection of medical books to try and understand what's happening, but I have changed. Now I go only to Christ and the Scriptures.

And I am not scared. I recently postponed a treatment to attend a youth group meeting of high school students who wanted to know what it's like to have a relationship with Christ while realizing you're soon going to die. That therapy was much more important to me than medication. I feel God's pleasure when I tell my story, and I know he will keep me alive long enough to do what I am here to do.

I believe love and compassion are the only things we can take with us when it's our time to go, and if we have only a little, we'll be nearly empty as we leave on our journey. *This* is the time to build up our supplies, and we have only a short time to make them grow. Still, if we use that time well, it's all the time we really need.

I believe it was Amy Carmichael who said, "We have only until sunset to secure victories we will celebrate for all of eternity." While the sun set on David's earthly life on May 27, 1998, the victories he won in the short time here will be trumpeted by heaven's choruses for billions upon billions of days, untouched by a single sunset. And even here, some of those victories can be celebrated.

For about fourty-five tearful minutes after his passing, David's family sat around his body and reminisced about the good times they had shared before his painful battle with cancer. When they all finished, one of his daughters got up, stood over the now-still body of her father, and said, "Now I get to hug my Daddy and it won't hurt him." And with that she gave her dad one final hug.

25

A HEAVENLY HEALING

When a woman is about to die, friends and family naturally focus on her needs, her comfort, her desires. Yet as Jo Brown faced her own imminent death, she focused not on her own suffering but on creative ways she could provide her family with precious memories that would sustain them through the dark days after her passing. She left behind not only a treasure trove of memories for her loved ones, but a potent example for all of us.

"When there's little hope, teach more cope."

That was the message Jo Brown enthusiastically preached to anyone threatened by early death. But she not only preached the message; she lived it out when she found herself facing a terminal illness.

In one sense, her personal confrontation with death began on June 12, 1996, when she was diagnosed with terminal ovarian cancer. Yet in another sense that journey already had begun years before with the deaths of her mother, two aunts, and a cousin from the same disease. In an effort to stave off the deadly plague, Jo had undergone a hysterectomy three years before her diagnosis. But when the doctor announced the frightening news that she had cancer, Jo didn't respond with bitterness or anger. Instead she determined to face this disease with the same courage and dignity she had displayed throughout her life.

Jo saw her mother suffer through intense chemotherapy and radiation treatments just four years before, and she knew immediately that such a harsh regimen wasn't for her. She wanted to die at home and so chose a local hospice program to help her family through the coming ordeal.

"As a family, we are dealing with it," she wrote of her cancer. "It is not going to defeat us. We are resting in Jesus and know we are in his will. I have such a peace about this. With the grand-children, and especially with 'Trapper' [Jo's oldest grandchild], I have been able to talk in detail about death being a natural part of life. We have cried together. He asks me questions I can't answer. Even Anna and 'Scooter' [two other grandkids], only two and one-half years old, comprehend that Jo is very sick. I've shown them where this cancer is located; where the needles go into my body. They know they have to rub me very lightly. Anna rubs my tummy every time she comes in and 'Scooter' will ask me, 'Jo Jo, are you well now? Can I drink after you?' We talk about this just like we talk about anything else so that we can deal with it."

Jo determined from the beginning that her affliction would not destroy either her spirit or her family. One poem by an unknown author especially ministered to her, and she often shared its words with interested listeners:

Cancer is so limited ...
It cannot cripple love,
It cannot shatter hope,
It cannot corrode faith,
It cannot eat away peace,
It cannot destroy confidence,
It cannot kill friendship,
It cannot shut out memories,
It cannot silence courage,
It cannot invade the soul,
It cannot reduce eternal life,
It cannot quench the Spirit,
It cannot lessen the power of the resurrection.

Shortly before she died, Jo arranged for her family's picture to be published in the *Anderson Independent-Mail* under the cap-tion, "Thanks, Anderson." The caption beneath the picture told her community, "You have indeed proven that Anderson is not only a great place to live, but a great place to die with dignity."

The community returned her affection, in spades. On July 20, 1996, Jo was honored with the first annual "Jo Brown Senior Citizens Day" at the Civic Center of Anderson. That date thereafter was to be observed annually as Senior Citizens Day in Anderson. At the celebration, South Carolina Lieutenant Governor Bob Peeler presented Jo with the Order of the Palmetto, the highest public service award given to citizens of the state. Many speakers lauded her work and character, including senior citizen Juanita Bowman, who said of Jo, "She brought sunshine into my life. She made everyone feel special and everyone loved her."[1] Another senior said Mrs. Brown "didn't show any partiality whether you were black or white or crippled or blind. A lot of people would say hello and keep on walking; she always had the time to listen."

This great outpouring of affection stemmed from Jo's work as the first Anderson County Senior Citizens Program Director, a position she held from 1984 to 1993. As head of the program she helped establish senior centers in five cities. Jo came to her love of seniors naturally, having been reared by a godly elderly aunt and uncle and grandparents after her young parents divorced. She said her foster parents gave her a love for life, the simple things, and a special affection for seniors. She married at age eighteen before she finished high school, but her husband was killed in an auto accident three weeks before she graduated; they had been married all of nine months. On June 7, 1968, she remarried when she and Paul Brown walked down the aisle.

Despite her early hardships, in her *Memories* journal written just before her death, Jo wrote, "I don't think I could ever have had a better life."

At the July 20 celebration, the Rev. J. O. Rich said to her, "Friend, you taught and are teaching us how to be a community. And now you're teaching us, as a community, how to die with dignity, power and healing."[2] He also said Jo was "the one person in

Anderson County who could bridge the gap between politics, race, and religion."

Representative John Tucker told the audience that day, "My grandmother told me long ago that the height of one's achievement is the giving of oneself. I don't know anybody who's given more than Jo Brown. She is a jewel and I love her."[3]

At the close of the program, Jo asked the community to look after her family when she was gone. She had good reason to believe the audience would honor her request. "Since my illness," she wrote, "I have not been alone. There has been a steady stream of friends taking care of me, cleaning my house, dressing me, preparing meals for the family, and doing all those things I can not do for myself now. I can't begin to tell you how many cards have been sent. God has allowed my family and friends to give me my flowers before my death through these many acts of kindness. I feel very blessed that God has allowed this time for me to help my family and friends deal with death and to help my grandchildren see that when you are dying, you can do it at home. It is so wonderful with your family and friends to love you and just to rest in Jesus."

Jo used her last summer on earth to prepare her family and friends for what she described as her "heavenly healing." As visitors poured into her home (called "Crooked Creek") laden with food, flowers, and words of comfort for Jo and her family, Jo greeted each one with her familiar, beautiful smile, and engaged each visitor in friendly conversation that inevitably focused on their lives, not on her illness. She encouraged many visitors to share a time of prayer and devotional reading before they left and had her picture taken with each visitor. She had duplicates made of every photo and sent the picture along with a special thank-you note to each person who spent time with her. Visitors often commented that they left Jo's home feeling refreshed, renewed, and strengthened by her strong faith, love of God, and love for each of them.

In her last months, Jo developed and managed systems to help those caring for her. She had a plan for everything: taking her medications, who would bring in what meal, what housework needed to be done, who had sent cards, who needed thank-you notes. Somehow she continued to attend worship services each Sunday during June, July, and August. She rarely complained of discomfort and insisted on doing things for herself as long as her strength allowed. She was very particular about her appearance; stylish hair, flawless makeup, and beautiful gowns were daily priorities.

Even as the end approached, Jo continued to think of others. For her husband's fiftieth birthday on August 16, she invited about seventy-five friends to her Crooked Creek home for homemade ice cream and cake. By then she struggled with any physical exertion, but for the party she dressed up in a stunning black dress, complete with matching jewelry. She waved from her upstairs bedroom window to the crowd who had gathered on the front lawn to wish Paul a Happy Birthday.

Jo's health declined dramatically after that day. She became confined to her downstairs couch and bedroom, lost her appetite, and was unable to keep food down. Friends tried to find some nourishment that her devastated system could digest; she laughingly referred to some of the drinks as "putracal" and "sustapuke." By the last week of her life she required round-the-clock care.

That week a remarkable event occurred which the family calls "Jo's Spiritual Awakening." Early on September 9, Jo rallied from her extremely frail condition to preach to her family and proclaim her love of Jesus. In a strong and assertive voice captured on video, Jo conveyed her hopes and directives to each family member and announced she was ready to go home. She said she saw her mansion and the heavenly light. The final minutes of the video record family members holding hands as they surround Jo's bed, in unison singing "Going Home."

Jo's final words to friends and family in her *Memories* journal express a similar message. "God has given me the strength to guide my family and friends through this eternal journey," she wrote on July 20, 1996. "May you, too, experience God's peace when you travel through the valley of the shadow of death. I love you forever and ever, Jo."

Jo Brown died on September 11, 1996. But before doing so, she helped design her own tombstone, which greets mourners with the faithful words of Psalm 56:3 that meant so much to Jo in her last days: "When I am afraid I put my trust in you." At a private burial service at "the resting place" on Crooked Creek, family members and friends said their last good-byes by releasing helium balloons and singing "I'll Fly Away."

While their friend, counselor, leader, and lover might be separated from them for a time, they knew her spirit lived on. And still they could hear the echo of her courageous and caring voice: "Cancer is a disease, but it is not a life sentence until God calls you home. You can make the most of every day. And that's what I have tried to do. I don't look beyond, just now. I take it one day at a time. God gives me the strength, fortitude, and quality of life. There are times when there is pain, but they are minimal times. Through all of this, I praise him. I acknowledge him, and I still want his will to be done.

I am not afraid of tomorrow
for I have lived yesterday,
and I love today."

Notes

1. Anna Simon, "Woman to receive Order of Palmetto," *The Greenville News,* July 18, 1996, 1D,2D.

2. Jenna Russell, "City celebrates life of altruist," *Independent-Mail,* July 21, 1996, 3A.

3. Russell

26

NOT UNTIL YOU'RE READY

The death of a young child is probably the most difficult trial any parent must endure. Paul and Tina D'Alessandro had to walk that excruciating path when their second son, James Paul (Jamie), was diagnosed in August 1996 with Stage 3 Burkitt's Lymphoma. Several rounds of intense chemotherapy followed and eventually doctors tried a bone marrow transplant. A family friend called the Outreach of Hope to ask for help. Toward the end of January 1997 I was able to speak to Jamie by telephone to encourage and pray with this brave little eight-year old. His small voice, made smaller by the morphine he was taking, made it clear to me that his body was growing weak. But Jamie and his mother still spoke with strong courage about what lay ahead.

Long before Tina D'Alessandro watched her son fight for life, she had lost her dad to cancer and her brother after an auto accident. Some ill-informed believers at the time said that since God never willed any Christian to die "prematurely," the deaths must have occurred because Tina and her family hadn't prayed enough or believed in God's power to heal. New to the faith, Tina wondered whether they might be right. Later she came to believe that such teachings were unbiblical and hurtful. And they did nothing to ease her fears about death.

When she became a mother, Tina always strove to be honest with Jamie and his brothers no matter what they asked. That policy didn't change once her son was diagnosed with cancer. Jamie trusted that her answers to his questions would be truthful—after all, his mom was a nurse.

Despite the diagnosis and prescribed treatments, the family enjoyed good times. The "Dreams Come True" foundation granted

Jamie his earnest request to see the New York Yankees play in Yankee Stadium—in fact, he was in the stands when the Yankees defeated the Atlanta Braves to win the 1996 World Series! A limousine picked up Jamie and his family members at the airport and delivered them to the Big Apple where they stayed for four magnificent days. During the game Jamie was escorted up to owner George Steinbrenner's private box and had his picture taken with the World Series trophy. He felt good the entire trip and, like any seven-year-old baseball fan, was thrilled at all the excitement surrounding the victory celebrations. Not even getting sick in the limo while returning to the airport could dim his enthusiasm for his big-city excursion.

Soon after his return from New York City, Jamie's health began to seriously decline. During Thanksgiving of 1996, Jamie relapsed and his doctors recommended the one option left to save his life: a bone marrow transplant. It didn't work. Two days after his eighth birthday, Jamie faced the grim reality that a medical cure was no longer possible. One day he looked at his mom and started crying. "That means I'm going to die," he whimpered. "No," Tina replied, "that means that the medicine can no longer help. Not one of us knows the exact moment that God will call us home to him. It means that it's time to go home and be together for as long as God has planned. He will either cure you while you're here with us or cure you when you go home to him."

To this point in her life, Tina—like most of us—harbored many fears and uncertainties about death. She had believed in Jesus' promise of everlasting life since she was a young girl, but the transition we call death always scared her. That all changed as her son prepared to leave this earth for heaven. Her fears and uncertainties were removed when she watched her son die with grace and complete trust in his parents and in God. Tina now sees death as a short journey, a simple trip from life on earth to our eternal home. But it took some remarkable events to burn this conviction into her heart.

"Mom," Jamie said, "I don't want to die. But if I do have to, I want you and Dad to go with me." Tina embraced her very ill son and responded, "Daddy and I want you to be with us, too." And then she made a promise that she hoped her Lord would make good: "God won't take you home until you're ready."

She asked God to comfort Jamie, his brothers, his father and her. She prayed for a cure for her son, but also for the grace to accept God's will regardless of what she felt to be best.

The second or third night home from the hospital after the failed transplant, Jamie very patiently told Tina, "Mom, you don't have to get up every time you hear me. Sometimes I'm just praying and talking to God. I'll call you if I need you." His dad overheard the conversation and asked him, "Does God talk back to you when you talk to him?" With a twinkle in his eye Jamie quietly explained, "Dad, I don't hear God with my ears. He answers me in my heart and I feel better."

Jamie was ecstatic to be with his family. He tired easily and could get cranky—especially with his exuberant younger brothers—but he was happy to be back home. He spent hours building Legos with his dad, sorting sports cards and filing them in their books, and following Duke basketball (since football season had ended for his beloved Jacksonville Jaguars). It wasn't until Friday, February 7, that Jamie's energy level declined drastically and Tina started feeling as if the end were approaching. Yet some important routines continued. Jamie still wanted his mom to read aloud to him; they were in the middle of the sixth book of C. S. Lewis' seven-volume *Chronicles of Narnia*. He also wanted to hear portions of Larry Libby's touching and sensitive children's book *Someday Heaven*.

By 3:00 A.M. Saturday Jamie's breathing became labored and from that moment on either Tina or Paul stayed constantly with their son. Jamie dozed on and off; he didn't talk a lot because breathing grew difficult, but he was awake and aware of activity swirling around him. By mid-afternoon Tina was lying on the bed next to Jamie, Paul was sitting on the end of the bed, his siblings played nearby, and "Nana" (Jamie's devoted grandmother) sat in the rocking chair. Suddenly, in a clear, loud and strong voice, Jamie looked at one corner of the ceiling and declared, "But I want to stay." He said nothing more.

"Are you talking to me or to one of us?" Tina asked him. He shook his head from side to side—NO. He closed his eyes to rest and the family was left to wonder if he had seen an angel or even Jesus himself. About 5:00 P.M. Jamie looked to the same corner of his ceiling and shouted, "GO AWAY!" Then once more he closed his eyes. Tina and Paul were the only other (visible) persons in the room at the time, and it was clear he was not talking to either of them.

Later that evening when the house grew still, Paul and Tina were discussing sleeping arrangements while Jamie quietly watched. Paul said Jamie's bedtime prayers with him while Tina showered. As she put socks on her cold feet, Paul called to her, "Tina, Jamie wants you." She could see both her son and her husband from where she was sitting but hadn't heard Jamie say a word, so she didn't rush or feel overly concerned. Tenderly Paul said again, "Tina, Jamie wants you. He squeezed my hand and I know he wants you."

As Tina entered Jamie's bedroom, he looked straight at her with both eyes wide open—a unique accomplishment since the cancer had made it impossible for him to open his right eye. When he saw his mom he shakily lifted both arms off the bed, open wide and palms up. *He was reaching for Jesus!* At last he was ready and he knew it was time to go.

Tina rushed to her son, scooped him up and held him close, her arms wrapped around him from behind; he was sitting in her lap. Paul held his hand as he took his last breath, relaxed into his mom, and let go. At that moment he left earth to be with his Lord.

"God won't take you home until you're ready," Tina had promised her son. Her mind often recalled the Lord's words in Isaiah 51:12—"I, even I, am he who comforts you . . . ." She had

spent the last week of Jamie's life praying that God would honor a mother's desperate words, spoken in love to her distressed son— and he did, gloriously.

Twice the King of the Universe listened to a little boy's plaintive call to be allowed to stay on earth for just a little while longer. Only when that boy was willing and ready to meet his heavenly Father was he summoned heavenward. Arms open wide, palms up, he went to sleep in his mother's embrace and in the next instant awakened to find the strong arms of God wrapped tightly around his no-longer-hurting body.

He was home. And not a moment too soon.

27

A MODEL FOR DYING

D r. Richard Strauss, the longtime pastor of Emmanuel Faith Community Church in Escondido, California, died in September 1993 from the effects of multiple myeloma, a form of bone marrow cancer. He discovered he had the disease four years before it finally took his life, and he used the time to prepare his family and his congregation for his imminent death.

If your doctor said you had only a few years to live, do you think it likely you would tell your dearest friends, "I want to model for you how to die, just as I have tried to model how to live"? I doubt most of us would express any such desire.

But then again, none of us is Dr. Richard Strauss.

On September 24, 1989, Dr. Strauss and Mary, his wife, explained to their church the long battle that lay ahead. At the time of the service Dr. Strauss didn't know all the struggles he would face in the next four years, but he knew he wanted to face them with strength and courage. In a service that oscillated between breathless silence and raucous laughter, Dr. Strauss, the pastor of Emmanuel Faith Community Church, stood before his beloved flock to make the following commitment:

"You know, it's been my desire, through my years of ministry with you, to show you how to live. I haven't always done that, believe me. People who know me best will tell you the most that I haven't always done that. But if God calls on me for an early exodus from this life, then by God's grace, my desire is to show you how to die. I want to model that. It may not be easy; I don't know what it's going to be like. This particular cancer can be painful, and I don't like pain. Quite frankly, I'm chicken when it comes to pain. But I know God's grace is sufficient. Just as my desire has been to show you how to live, my desire at that point will be to show you how to die. And I trust God will allow me to have that privilege, if that is his will."

The privilege was granted.

Dr. Strauss's painful odyssey began about a year before his diagnosis. He noticed that his ribs would "pop" when he'd play with his grandkids or when he'd reach for some item just out of reach. By August 1989 these incidents grew worrisome and he was scheduled for a battery of tests. Within days he learned he had multiple myeloma, a form of cancer that destroys the bones and makes them brittle. "You could break a bone by unscrewing a lid off a jar," his doctor warned him. While the disease could be treated, it could not be cured. Death would come either by kidney failure or by infections that a weakened immune system could no longer fight. Dr. Strauss was told the average life expectancy for someone at his stage of the disease was four years; some had lived up to fifteen years, while others had lasted less than two.

After recovering from the news, Dr. Strauss began to think about John 10:4, the "Great Shepherd" text. As the Great Shepherd, Jesus went before his sheep and so encountered everything that would confront his flock. Dr. Strauss applied this idea to himself as the "undershepherd" of a growing flock. "I consider this a privilege to experience some of the things many of you have or will experience in days to come," he told his church. "As the shepherd, the Lord has given me the opportunity to go before you and hopefully, to relate to you better and minister to you more effectively."

"God is trusting us with this," added Mary. "Pray that we will be faithful to this trust, whether by life or death."

Cancer—a "privilege," a "trust"? How often have you heard someone call it that? Yet that's what Dr. Strauss called it, and he meant it. Still, he would fight to the last to stay in this world as long as possible. Soon after being diagnosed he began chemotherapy; by the third year of his illness, his hair fell out. From the beginning, he and Mary had joked about this day and privately debated whether he should wear a wig or go bald. Mary wanted to put the decision up to a vote of the congregation, but Dr. Strauss nixed that idea and said he'd wear a wig.

As the months wore on, his body began to deteriorate. Markedly. He lost three inches of height due to the multiplying and painful compressed fractures in his spine. He told one group of missionary candidates, "It doesn't take a lot for me to say, 'Oh, boy. Do I have to put up with this again?' Every time something new happens—like the pain in my ribs this week—I have to work through it again. I'll think I'm making progress, but then I realize, 'No, I'm not. I'm deteriorating.'"[1]

The cancer that was eating away his body could not touch his soul, however, and a big part of that soul reveled in a lively sense of humor. A member of Emmanuel gave Dr. Strauss and his wife a new car, a Nissan Infiniti, but the pastor could not drive it because of the high doses of morphine he took to ease his increasing pain. Not long before he died, Dr. Strauss cut back his pain medications and so at last was able to drive his car—and he and Mary joked that soon one of them would be in eternity and the other in the Infiniti.

"It's not wrong to weep and it's not wrong to sorrow," Dr. Strauss told his congregation at the beginning of his battle with cancer, "but we don't sorrow as others who have no hope. That's the difference. That hope mellows and moderates our sorrow and our grief, and it puts an altogether different light on it. Yes, there will be hard times. And yes, I enjoy being here and I enjoy my ministry. But if God chooses to take me home, we're going to rejoice even in that, because as the apostle Paul put it, that's far better. This is a messy old world, folks, and I have a better home."

Some Christians say it's foolish and wrong to talk about one's own death, but Dr. Strauss rejected that kind of thinking. "Some people think that even talking about the possibility of death is a lack of trust," he told his rapt audience the night he explained his battle with multiple myeloma. "I don't see it that way at all. I think it takes more trust, actually, than to say, 'God's going to heal! Don't even talk about dying!' I believe God can heal. But I also know God doesn't *always* heal. You don't have to look very far to see that, friends. We can pray for healing and we want you to pray for healing. *Total* healing. But don't demand that from God. Always pray, 'God, if it be your will.' When Jesus faced that awful pain of the cross, he said, 'If it be possible, take this cup from me. Nevertheless, not my will, Lord, but yours be done.' And we want God's will more than we want our will. We want Christ to be magnified by life or by death."

In the case of Dr. Richard Strauss, it was death.

When he first learned of his terminal diagnosis, Dr. Strauss said his wife's "life verse," Philippians 1:20, leapt to mind: "I eagerly expect and hope that I will in no way be ashamed, but will have sufficient courage so that now as always Christ will be exalted in my body, whether by life or by death." As his health worsened, Dr. Strauss sought radical treatment at the Arkansas Cancer Research Center in Little Rock, Arkansas, where he underwent a stem-cell transplant.[2] In October 1992, he and Mary flew to Little Rock for the first part of the procedure, the harvesting of healthy stem cells. Three months later they returned for the first of two planned transplants. The procedure went very well and doctors believed that with another transplant the following September, Dr. Strauss might gain two more years of life.

But it was not to be. By the time he returned to Little Rock in September 1993, his ravaged body could no longer handle the stress of the severe treatments. He died at the hospital, surrounded by his wife and four sons, two of whom had returned to the United States from missionary service in Africa.

Throughout his illness, Dr. Strauss had continued to preach, preparing his sermons six to eight weeks in advance. He never got to preach the last one he wrote, titled "Following God in the Dark." In it, he wrote,

"We believers sometimes find ourselves in situations marked by danger, difficulty, and uncertainty. We don't really know what's happening. It would be a comfort to us to be assured that somebody who knows more than we know is looking out for us and directing us. If we knew that, we might be willing to trust him and follow him even in the dark places when we have no idea where he's taking us."

One of Dr. Strauss's favorite promises is found in 2 Corinthians 2:14, his own life verse: *"But thanks be to God, who always leads us in His triumph in Christ, and manifests through us the sweet aroma of the knowledge of Him in every place" (NASB). He died confident that even though cancer could defeat his mortal body, his Lord would lead him in triumph for eternity. Even in death he displayed the courage he longed to manifest ever since he first learned of his awful disease.*

Dr. Strauss had taught his flock how to live, and now he had taught them how to die. How could a ministry be more complete?

Notes

1. David L. Goetz, "The Death of a Preacher," *Leadership*, Winter 1994, Volume XV, Number 1, page 128.

2. In a stem-cell transplant, a patient's stem cells are harvested and frozen, then reintroduced into the patient's body a few months later. (Stem cells produce baby bone marrow, which is free of myeloma.) While harvesting the stem cells is a relatively simple procedure, reintroducing them into the patient's body can be quite dangerous. The patient first undergoes high doses of chemotherapy and radiation to kill off as much of the myeloma as possible, then the stem cells are reintroduced in an effort to stimulate the production of healthy bone marrow.

28

STAY STEADY

No one welcomes a diagnosis of terminal cancer, but such a medical declaration at least provides the patient with advance warning that it's time to put one's affairs in order. While all of us will die, most of us don't know when. Jim Andrews did.

Both Jim and his wife, Leslie, had volunteered their time at the Outreach of Hope to minister to those afflicted by cancer or amputation. That didn't change when Jim was diagnosed with malignant melanoma. And neither did Jim's commitment to care for his family and loved ones after his death. His life was a constant testament to faithfulness. Jim was a unique man full of practical wisdom and deep compassion, and it was our overwhelming pleasure to get to know him before he left this earth. It's also my pleasure to tell you his story in the hope that it will encourage all of us to reach out to others, regardless of circumstances.

"It's not good," the doctor told Jim Andrews, a godly husband and the father of three young boys. "The melanoma has spread into your brain and we have no treatment for that. You're going to die."

Jim had been battling this life-threatening disease for seven years, and two days before he received the doctor's chilling news he had been given a contradictory report suggesting he had been cured. That's why neither Jim nor his wife, Leslie, were prepared to hear the dreaded prognosis. Despite the devastating news, Jim never lost his composure at that meeting. In calm and measured tones, he patiently asked four questions of the doctor sitting just three feet away:

"How long do I have to live?" Answer: three months.

"What will my symptoms look like?" Answer: seizures, nausea, headaches.

"Can I still take a planned trip to Disney World with our children?" Answer: Probably, but only if you refuse any life-extending treatment.

"Do I have time to take care of things at home before the symptoms make that impossible?" Answer: You have about six weeks.

The bottom line for Jim was that he had only twelve or so weeks to live, half of which he would feel all right, the other half he would become progressively weaker and sicker.

Jim and Leslie drove home that afternoon in silence. After nearly an hour of quiet disturbed only by the hum of the car's engine, Leslie asked her husband, "What are you thinking?"

"As we were leaving the hospital," Jim replied, "I silently asked, 'God, what is going on?' All I heard in reply was, 'Jim, stay steady.'"

That phrase had been God's word to Jim for several weeks prior to his diagnosis, and it became the foundation on which Jim built the last few weeks of his life. Stay steady. Don't try any heroics. Don't change everything now. Stay on the track you have followed all these years. *Stay steady.*

When a husband and father receives a medical death sentence, his mortality immediately confronts him. Life becomes precious and the time left to him seems golden. Material things lose their luster and eternal things come into sharp focus. It certainly was that way for Jim Andrews.

The first "practical" thing he did was to close his business. He had worked as a real estate appraiser for seventeen years and his clients loved him. One by one he phoned each of them with the terrible news. "It was so hard to walk into the office after that," Leslie said. "We loved the people who worked for Jim and his partner. Facing them was painful. They adored Jim and you could see the hurt in their eyes as they visited with us."

Jim calmly decided against any further treatments aimed at extending his life a few months. The harsh chemotherapy regimen he already had undergone had taken its toll, and he and his doctors decided it would be best to spend his last energies enjoying his wife and children. He did not want to extend his life at the expense of truly living.

The Andrews family took a planned trip to Disney World, enjoying a beautiful week at the park, then another three days by the Gulf of Mexico. As Jim played and splashed with his boys in the ocean, God kept away any dark thoughts such as, *Could this be the last time. . . ?* Even so, it was an emotional trip. Jim took every opportunity to hug and hold and touch his boys, locking onto them emotionally while never smothering them or making them feel uncomfortable. Leslie took a picture of each of their three boys playing in the surf alone with their dad. The photos might not win a prize, but they're precious nonetheless. Everyone had a great time and stored away scores of priceless memories.

But the inevitable eventually took its course. Leslie said, "We knew that without a miracle, Jim would soon die. So we prayed for our miracle but had to live with the practical issues of tears, confusion, and Jim's growing weakness. We talked of life and God, of death and hope, and of our family's future. If he couldn't remain with us, Jim wanted to know we would be cared for. So he wrote letters to a select group of twenty-four trusted friends, asking them to pray, offer counsel, fix leaky faucets, and build close relationships with his sons after his death. I was dumbfounded when he first approached me with this idea. He was dying, and yet his major concern was to provide for us!"

His major concern, but not his only one. Jim had Leslie drive him to the Outreach of Hope so he could pray for the ministry's needs. And he did pray, each day, earnestly. Rather than allow his life to be defined by what cancer took from him, Jim measured his days by what he gave through prayer.

Still, Jim's family remained his primary concern. In his last four months of life, Jim labored over a letter to his three sons, Daniel, Taylor, and Kevin. It became a true work of art as the pages unfolded a father's deep, deep love for his sons, his bright hopes for their future, instructions for living without him, and his broken heart at having to leave them. He encouraged his boys to commit their lives to Christ's control, challenged them to live clean, honest, and morally strong lives, and even asked them to allow Leslie to rebuild her life and perhaps remarry when the time was right. Jim wrote that letter while fighting seizures, headaches, nausea, and pain. He finished it just two weeks before his death. The letter is now a treasure to Jim's three boys, who read it now and then just to "touch" their dad.

Jim also began a letter to Leslie which he never finished. In it he reaffirmed his deep love for her and expressed his gratitude that he could identify no past hurts or conflicts that had to be resolved from their sixteen years of delightful marriage. "I wish I had the rest of that letter," Leslie admits. "But in my heart I know what we shared was good and pure. The commitment we made at the altar in 1978 stood life's supreme test. 'Till death do us part' just came much too soon."

As Jim's headaches and seizures grew more frequent and severe, he decided to move out of the house and into a hospice facility. "I still don't know what he was thinking as he left home for the last time," Leslie said. "I can only imagine the heartache he must have felt, as we silently drove past homes and neighborhoods he'd passed hundreds of times, but knowing he would never see them again."

Jim died on September 15, 1994, and on that day Leslie lost her friend, her companion, her lover, and one of the most precious people she ever was gifted to know. She describes the years since his death as a "roller coaster ride" and says "the pain often reaches up from nowhere and clutches my heart. I must stop, face the moment, express the agony, and then get back to the business of living." And yet her memories of Jim are precious beyond words.

"I believe Jim knew how deeply my losing him would affect me," she said. "I believe he knew the pain would sear my heart and almost destroy me before I came through the valley and could begin to live again. Knowing this, he did everything in his power to smooth the way. He faced every obstacle he could identify and tried to deal with each one before he left us. He was a living example of love, grace, and peace—truly, a living sacrifice poured out for those whom he loved. He is the closest I have come to seeing Jesus alive in this world."

"What is your life?" *the New Testament writer James asks us. "You are a mist that appears for a little while and then vanishes"* (James 4:14). *Jim Andrews understood that none of us has a guarantee of tomorrow. Our lives really are just vapors.*

Yet this isn't all bad. Often it's just this realization that causes us to turn to God for answers. And if the uncertainty of life here below leads us to the certainty of life above, we will have found the biggest prize of all. Like Jim Andrews, I've read the Bible and I know one thing for sure: There are no mists in heaven.

In Psalm 90:12 Moses wrote, "Teach us to number our days aright, that we may gain a heart of wisdom." The Lord certainly answered that prayer in the life of Jim Andrews. Jim was lucky in the sense that he knew his days were soon coming to an end, and he used his remaining time to care for his family and to prepare for eternity. We could do a lot worse than to follow his example.

29

FREE AT LAST

In our devotional Do Not Lose Heart, *Jan and I briefly describe the plight of Tom Moore.[1] Suffering seemed to be a way of life for Tom. When we met him, he was in a final round of suffering. As he lay in bed, unable to do much of anything any longer, he held tight to the fact that he was soon "going home." He believed in God's promise of heaven, and that potent hope sustained him and gave him the strength to endure whatever time on earth he had left.*

When we meet people who face death with grace and strength, we naturally want to label them courageous and brave. Yet often when these people hear such words attached to their names, they object. Tom Moore was one such person.

"While I am not fearful of death, I do not see myself as a brave person," Tom wrote shortly before he died. "I only know that when I am walking hand in hand with Jesus, things are better. I have terrible times of weakness, and in those times all I want is for him to take me home. My personal history has left me with no long-term roots and I long for that place where I can find continuous peace, a place where justice and love are the norm. I just want to walk with Jesus down that brightly lit tunnel that leads to the place where love reigns. I long for a place where I am free of pain after so many years. The place we call heaven."

Tom's life was never easy and he had to claw a long way up just to reach level ground. His mother died when he was four, and "everything fell to pieces." His father's poor health forced him to pass along Tom and his siblings from relative to relative; eventually all three wound up in foster homes. The father in one of these homes—a rigid, religious man—often got drunk and in alcohol-induced rages whipped Tom with a plastic belt, leaving him badly cut up. When Tom's biological father discovered the whippings, he placed his children in another foster home, one that already had five or six children. Tom remembered this home as "mostly a place to eat and sleep. We just ran the streets." Tom frequently stood by the front door, waiting in his pea coat and cowboy hat for a father who almost never visited. "This part really hurt and still does to this day," Tom wrote. "I wish I knew why he didn't come."

Eventually Tom's father remarried and reunited his family, but eighteen months later he was dead. Tom's stepmother adopted the kids in 1955 and the family entered a stage of extreme poverty and frequent hunger. Tom remembered going barefoot all one summer, even to church, for lack of shoes. He went to work at age thirteen and for two and a half years delivered milk on a route truck. For $1.25 per morning, he rose at 4:30 A.M. and returned home in time for school. Out of his $7 weekly earnings, Tom bought all his clothes, glasses, school supplies, and any "extras" he wanted (precious few of these).

Tom called this period of his life his "religious childhood"— church three times a week and innumerable rules. It seemed to Tom that everywhere he went, someone was watching him. He soon learned a very twisted view of God. "I have no childhood memories of a loving God," he wrote. "To me, he was someone to be feared, someone who was always watching for every little mistake, with harsh judgment to follow." These were years of fear, getting in trouble, and subpar performance in school.

Tom's stepmother remarried during his fifteenth year; her new husband suffered from multiple handicaps and was unemployable. Tom's sister hated the new home and ran away, entering a string of disastrous marriages. The family moved three times in nine months, finally winding up in San Angelo, Texas.

After graduating from high school, Tom married his longtime sweetheart. But the marriage was anything but smooth. "We merged brokenness," Tom explained simply. He spent twelve years in the naval reserve and finally was discharged due to a back injury suffered during a training weekend. (He later underwent three serious back surgeries.) His wife miscarried their first child just a few days before Tom was released from active duty in June 1969, and the bereaved family moved to Memphis, Tennessee. There his son Tom was born six weeks prematurely. He suffered from several complications and spent the first two weeks of his life in the hospital.

Tom later took his family back to west Texas and worked for a year in a residential program for behaviorally disordered children aged twelve to twenty. Then another move, this time to Odessa, Texas, where Tom became program director of an alternative learning center. At the same time he began graduate school in marriage and family counseling, and adopted a second son, Jared. Within months of taking a new job in Wichita, his marriage disintegrated and his wife divorced him. Tom then wandered into "New Age stuff"—channeling, tarot cards, astrology, crystals. "It seemed to be fun reading other people's minds," he confessed.

Tom moved to Vandenburg, California, joined a local chapter of Parents without Partners, and there met Alice, "the love of my life." Within a few years of their marriage, a third back operation finally ended Tom's working career.

Yet good things also began happening. Alice helped Tom discover inner healing by relying on Jesus in prayer to free himself from heavy burdens of the past. Tom soon felt called to ministry and enrolled at Fuller Seminary. For two and a half years he took classes and attended a wonderful church, Silverlake, where he said his inner healing was completed. "God has guided me in unknown ways *all of my life*," he wrote. "Long before I knew him, he was guiding, protecting, and leading me. Especially, he was loving me. It amazes me to think how he loved me. When I think of the way I should have ended up, it is incredible."

Tom and Alice left Fuller as part of a team determined to plant a church for unchurched people in Phoenix, but there Tom's health began to deteriorate. In 1987 he started suffering with nausea, vomiting, and diarrhea, with lower left abdominal pain for weeks at a time. He felt sick for most of three years while doctors scrambled unsuccessfully to discover the cause of his suffering. Yet he was grateful for the change in his spiritual outlook.

"After a childhood and many years thereafter of knowing only fear of God, to have some fifteen years of knowing a God who loves me and cares for me, has given me peace and a strength to face what comes," he wrote. "I don't know how I could have made it without Jesus. I'm sure I would have killed myself, because during the three years while they were looking for my illness, I went through a phase where I was actively suicidal. I confessed the problem to our Wednesday night prayer and praise group. They stopped the service and gathered around and prayed for me. I felt a sense of peace, but not much else. The next day about noon, I realized the desire was gone. It has never returned and I have been much sicker since that time. God healed me of any desire to take my own life."

After three years of searching for a diagnosis, a CT scan eventually revealed a cancerous tumor. It turned out to be islet cell cancer, a very rare, slow-growing pancreatic tumor. His case was terminal. The standard treatments of chemotherapy and radiation don't work with this disease. Surgery is the only option and Tom soon faced several operations.

Tom and Alice then moved to Fresno, California, to be closer to family. They found a solid church, but Tom's illness soon made it impossible for him to attend. He was often forced to stay home alone, and he found this the most difficult part of his ordeal. "As I lose more and more functions, it gets harder and harder to maintain composure," he wrote. "Sometimes I just want to scream, 'You don't understand. You can't possibly know what it is like to watch your life just ebb away.'

"As I have become much sicker, I simply want Jesus to come and take me to that place where there is no pain and bodies work the way God designed them. I'm sorry, but after living with pain from cancer for more than nine years and chronic back pain for more than twenty years, when I am really hurting I will cry out, 'God, please take me. Set me free from the pain.' Someday (soon, I hope) I will join that heavenly choir and sing with them. I will be free of pain and suffering for eternity and say with all my heart, 'free at last, free at last, thank God Almighty, I'm free at last.'"

Tom didn't have long to wait. He died on May 21, 1997. Among his last words were these: "I don't know whether the time left is days or weeks. I just know I am very tired. . . . My friends in Jesus, thanks for loving me, carrying me when needed, but most of all for being there. I don't leave much in a tangible way, but I have been blessed with some special people who I know I will see again."

At the very end, Tom's family gave him permission to go home to his Lord. He had lapsed into a coma, but just before he died he came out of it, picked up his head, and opened his eyes. Immediately his deathly pallor vanished. Alice firmly believes that, at that moment, her husband came face to face with the living hope he had banked on through all his years of suffering. And she remembered his confident words written just weeks before his relocation to heaven: "I believe in a God of grace and when the time comes for me to go to my real home, God will accept my best efforts." Without any doubt, that last exuberant look on his face confirmed his most confident expectations.

Notes

1. From the vignette "As Good As Dead" in *Do Not Lose Heart* by Dave and Jan Dravecky (Grand Rapids, MI: Zondervan Publishing House, 1998), page 68, 69.

30

A TENDER GOOD NIGHT

*W*e never want to say a permanent goodbye to our loved ones. Not to a parent, and especially not to a son or daughter. But in the story of Diana Trundle, two women—one a daughter, the other a mother—had to do both. Elizabeth Jessup, Diana's daughter, remembers.

Mom and Grandma were so much alike. They both worked hard taking care of themselves and their homes. They both received their greatest joy in being mothers and grandmothers. My grandmother is now a great-grandmother and I always assumed my mother would also one day become a great-grandmother. Both Mom and Grandma shared a common faith in Jesus Christ and devoted themselves to God in prayer and worship.

At eighty-nine, Grandma was still in amazingly good health. Her robust physical condition was part of the reason I was so shocked when doctors told my sixty-four-year-old mom that she had inoperable lung cancer and had only six months to a year to live.

I always felt a special closeness to my mother and grandmother. I was my mother's firstborn and Grandma was there at Mom's side during my delivery; in fact, Grandma was the first person to see me after I entered the world. So I wondered how Grandma felt as she sat by my mother's side once again, thirty-eight years later.

I know Grandma wished that it could have been her time to go and not Mom's. Though it must have distressed my grandmother to see her "baby" in such a deteriorated condition, Grandma brought a quiet sense of reassurance into the room—like all was going to be OK because "Mommy is here." I watched her grasp my mother's hand and noticed for the first time how even their hands looked similar; they fit perfectly together. Grandma released Mom from any obligation to speak and declared that she and "Di" didn't need any words because they shared a special bond; they just understood each other. It was true. They communicated more in that gentle grasp than words could ever express.

During the early morning hours of July Fourth I was awakened by my uncle and aunt who were keeping the night vigil. Mom had taken a dramatic turn for the worse and was suffering a severe episode of respiratory distress. I was frightened, but we tried to make Mom as comfortable as possible. She was on .25 cc of morphine and a pill that was supposed to reduce the panic of being unable to breathe, yet nothing seemed to work. I know that panic, for I have an allergic condition which can result in anaphylactic shock. When breathing is restricted, the body automatically panics and violently claims its need for more oxygen. It is frightening to experience, but perhaps more frightening to see someone you love go through it. Finally, after several hours of battling for every breath, Mom fell asleep, exhausted.

Hours later she awoke, only to suffer even more severe respiratory distress. She kept saying she needed to go and would try to rise out of her bed. We didn't know if she needed to use the restroom, was disoriented, or perhaps knew her time to depart was coming. I knew I was in way over my head and called for the hospice nurse and my mother's priest to come quickly.

I told Mom the nurse had authorized an increase in her morphine level to 3 cc. She shook her head and emphatically whispered, ".75, only .75. I want to be alert for when Father arrives." Mom had been a nurse and worked until the day she was diagnosed. We teased her that she was still orchestrating medical care even as a patient!

A short while later our family celebrated communion around Mom's bedside. There was something so familiar about this, and yet so very strange. I had never taken communion with death hovering so close by. At first it seemed contradictory—"celebrating" communion with death as the backdrop? But then I realized I had never enjoyed a more authentic communion experience. The very first communion is often called Jesus' Last Supper—last because Jesus knew his death was only hours away. Yet he broke bread and shared the cup with his loved ones. He had gone before us, even in this painful event. I was so grateful for that kind of love from Jesus, yet I felt agony at the thought that Mom soon would be taken from us.

Mom never complained. Only once did I hear her softly plead to God under her breath, "Let's not do it like this." My heart broke for her. I felt as if I had heard a whisper from the Garden of Gethsemane: "If this cup can pass from me. . .nevertheless not my will, but yours be done." Mom yielded to the Father's will and bravely faced what she did not want to experience.

The time came when Mom had to sit upright in bed just to get a gulp of air. Grandma, my brother and aunt were at her bedside on her left. My uncle was behind her, helping her to sit up. My other aunt and sister were on her right side, also assisting in the effort to prop her up. I was at her feet so she could see me as I spoke words of encouragement.

I knelt there, watching Mom make the sign of the cross, and suddenly realized that I had arrived at the foot of the cross itself. As I saw Mom slowly suffocate, I remembered that death on the cross also came that way. The hanging position of the condemned man required him to push up his body with his feet in order to free up his diaphragm for another breath. Roman guards often grew impatient with this slow execution and sped it up by breaking the legs of the condemned. Now, as my mom had to sit up a little taller for each breath, I realized she was sharing in the sufferings of Christ (Colossians 1:24).

Mom grew exceedingly tired from her continual state of respiratory distress. She wanted desperately to rest, yet every time her head touched the pillows (now propped up and held high so that she had only to tilt her head to rest) she would awake immediately in a panic. None of us seemed able to do anything to help Mom relax. And then a beautiful scene unfolded.

Somewhere between two and three o' clock in the afternoon, my grandmother, seeing her daughter's exhaustion, traveled back in her mind to retrieve a ritual the two of them had shared thousands of times. Grandma held my mother's hand and said, "Now Di, this is your Momma." Mom paid attention; you could see that beautiful connection of love they shared was fully alive even as Mom was dying. "Remember when you were a little girl and I would stroke you just like this before I put you to bed every night?" Grandma then performed that sweet bedtime ritual that every mother uniquely creates with her children. My mother visibly relaxed with the familiar routine and leaned in toward my grandmother. "Well, honey," Grandma continued, "you're so very tired right now. It's time for you to go to sleep." She continued stroking Mom's arm and sweet, bald head. Like an obedient child, Mom complied and said, "All right, Mom."

My grandmother had given my mom permission to go—the sweetest gift a mom could give her dying daughter. Mom then began saying a tender good night to everyone in the room, by name, and in turn we all wished her a good night. This went on for perhaps an hour. And then she closed her eyes and fell asleep.

Close to 5:00 P.M. Mom's breathing changed. My grandmother sensed the end was approaching and cried out in anguish, "My baby . . ."

Mom's spirit left her body at 5:30 P.M. on July 4, 1996. I left the house to be alone and visited the chapel where she often went to pray. I thanked God that Mom died on the Fourth of July. I have always held July 4 as a special holiday; my class graduated during our nation's bicentennial. Now there would be added meaning to the holiday. It would be Mom's day of independence, the day she was freed from her battle with cancer.

As Elizabeth's family silently watched the fireworks that evening, she felt as if heaven itself were celebrating her mom's arrival home. To Elizabeth, the explosion of lights in the darkness seemed to symbolize her mother's death. She says that in years to come, fireworks will always prompt her to look up to heaven and remember her country's freedom, bought by the death of dear patriots—but even more, they will remind her of her dear mother, who through death showed her the freedom we have in Christ. His light pierces even the darkness of disease and death and will surely lead us home.

For further information on Dave Dravecky's Outreach of Hope and its ministry to cancer patients and amputees, please write to:

Dave Dravecky's Outreach of Hope
13840 Gleneagle Dr.
Colorado Springs, CO 80921

For speaking engagements, please contact Barb Reynolds at:
Alive Communications
1465 Kelly Johnson Blvd.
Suite 320
Colorado Springs, CO 80920

Stand by Me
A Guidebook of Practical Ways to Encourage a Hurting Friend

"I want to help but I don't know how." If you've ever been close to someone who's hurting, you know the feeling. What do you say? What don't you say?

This small, practical book provides guidance for helping and encouraging a friend or loved one in their time of pain. It's also for the hurting, framing their experiences in words they can relate to. Drawn from a variety of sources, each page offers a fresh perspective on comfort and encouragement, a way to stand by the hurting, pairing one insightful writing with a quote or verse from Scripture.

This jewel-like book makes a wise companion for people who care— and for those who, in the midst of their pain, will appreciate the quick doses of comfort so abundant here.

Softcover 0-310-21646-X

Do Not Lose Heart
Meditations of Encouragement and Comfort

"Therefore we do not lose heart. Though outwardly we are wasting away, yet inwardly we are being renewed day by day. For our light and momentary troubles are achieving for us an eternal glory that far outweighs them all. So we fix our eyes not on what is seen, but what is unseen. For what is seen is temporary, but what is unseen is eternal."
—2 Corinthians 4:16–18

Suffering will touch us all sooner or later. It may be personal pain or it may be the pain of someone we're close to. Dave and Jan Dravecky understand suffering. Dave's bout with cancer that resulted in the removal of his left arm and Jan's dark valley of depression that only God's grace could lift are the experiences that give them credibility when they tell hurting people, Do Not Lose Heart.

Based on the Scripture passage that has become the Draveckys' motto, 2 Corinthians 4:16–18, this book of meditations is for people who are struggling and need just a few wise, uplifting words to lift their spirits— words from fellow Christians who know what it's like. Contributors to this book include Dave and Jan, Joni, C. H. Spurgeon, D. L. Moody, C.S. Lewis, and Oswald Chambers.

The book also features the luminous artwork of internationally renowned painter Thomas Kinkade, the "Painter of Light." A feast for the eye and the heart, Do Not Lose Heart is the perfect comfort and encouragement for anyone who suffers or grieves.

Hardcover 0-310-21706-7

Glimpses of Heaven

*Reflections on Your
Eternal Hope*

The journey of suffering brings with it a longing for heaven. For those who want encouragement for their journey, this gem of a book (a companion to *Stand by Me*) will lighten the load and remind them of their heavenly hope.

This book is an uplifting collection of quotes and comments about heaven, laced with the powerful encouragement of Scripture. Drawing together the words of writers, theologians, humorists, and even children, this little book offers insight into that place of promise and hope, heaven.

Those who are facing difficult times—illness, grief, loss, suffering of any kind—will find ready encouragement and assurance in these pages. Optimistic yet willing to look at the difficulty of dealing with sorrow and pain, *Glimpses of Heaven* makes a wonderful gift for the ill or dying, reminding them of the promise of their eternal, heavenly home.

Hardcover 0-310-21626-5

A Joy I'd Never Known
*One Woman's Triumph Over
Panic Attacks and Depression*

For Jan Dravecky, joy came after
she released control of her life . . .
into the hands of the God who had been waiting to receive it.

This book traces Jan's painful journey from control to surrender, winding from her protected childhood through a series of tragic losses, her
husband's cancer and the amputation of his arm, the downward spiral
of a devastating clinical depression, the lack of understanding on the
part of fellow Christians, and finally, to hope, growth, and joy as Jan
found the help she needed.

Jan's gripping, personal story sheds much-needed light on depression,
anxiety attacks, and the need for a balanced, surrendered lifestyle. And
for all who feel the lingering shame of emotional trauma or the need to
"keep it all together" at any cost, this book offers empathy and hope
for change . . . and points the way to joy beyond imagination.

Softcover 0-310-21941-8